MW01228124

Dedicated to
The memory of my Dad
'Frank (Bob) Jones'

"Sow for yourselves righteousness; reap steadfast love; break up your fallow ground, for it is the time to seek the Lord, that he may come and rain righteousness upon you."
Hosea 10:12 ESV

A Plowman prepares the field, so the sower can plant the seed.

'Holy Spirit, break up the fallow ground that the implanted word may take root. Amen.'

THE PLOWMAN

My Journey of God's Threefold Mercy

A Memoir By Michael 'Mo' Jones

CHAPTER 1
"IT BEGINS"

Identity As a Bass Player
(1979-1987)

Thanks Dad

He had the best baritone voice I've ever heard, and I remember hearing him sing as a child, thinking he was a rock star. It seemed like he was always singing everywhere we went, and he did not care who was around. I remember when we would go up to Timber Shores which is somewhere near Traverse City, Michigan, and he was always leading songs around the campfire- even the ones he made up, "Cluster 44" for those who remember that song. I just remember that he wasn't afraid to sing and express himself as a singer. This would be his habit throughout my upbringing and even into my adult years. He would sing at the kitchen sink or while driving down the road.

Where I really heard him sing with his biggest heart was in church. He would belt out those hymns like nobody's business, especially around Christmas time. He sparked something in me to pursue music and make it my life. Little did he know that he was planting seeds of music in me every time he would spontaneously break out in song, sing songs around a campfire, or sing those hymns in church. Music is my life today and I am so thankful for my dad's zeal for singing and not being timid to share his voice with those around him. Thanks Dad! I will see you soon - rest in peace.

Where It Started

It was very evident that I loved music. I started piano lessons early at the age of 7. This was a great start to developing a love for music. Hearing the melody in the right hand along with the bass in the left hand was showing me how music worked. After a few years I found a couple guitars lying around the house. Probably used to be my brothers or something, anyway, I would pick up those guitars and doodle. I really started to like the guitar more than the piano. I discovered bar chords and would mess around with my own chords. I switched to the guitar and started taking guitar lessons from a guy named

Bud at Shores Music in Flint, Michigan.

In the neighborhood where I grew up, there were 5 of us young kids who would get together and hangout. It was pretty cool because in doing so, that the five of us were becoming good friends. There was Craig, James, Adrian, Jack and me. We loved to play football and hide and seek throughout the neighborhood. As a young boy I also developed a love for the sport of bowling. Craig and I were on a bowling league together, and that is how we grew to become best friends. I remember at that age I so wanted to become a pro bowler. I loved the crack of those bowling pins when throwing a strike. It was an exciting rush.

Then one day Craig had this idea to form a neighborhood band. I just started playing the guitar, but Craig and James had already been playing it. Jack played drums and Adrian sang and played a little guitar. I really didn't know that there was all this musical talent in the neighborhood! We played together outside a lot- hide and seek, throw stones at bats, build tree forts- and to my surprise we didn't hurt ourselves. In all of that, none of us knew the others had any musical talent.

This idea to rock the world took all of us by storm. We wanted to be just like the rockers we would listen to, and tour the world. Now, four out of five of us played guitar, so someone had to play the bass. Because I was easy to push around, the other band members strong-armed me into playing the bass guitar. I really didn't want to play bass because there was a saying back then in the music scene that 'if you played bass, it's because you couldn't handle the guitar.' Like you weren't smart enough to figure it out. I was bummed out because I believed I would be tagged as one who couldn't handle the guitar, so I had to play bass. Even with that stigma, I accepted this new role as the bass player. I just wanted to do music, so I told the guys that I would play bass. I kinda looked at it as I wanted to still be in the band, and every band we listened to had a bass player, so I would be that bass player. I felt like I was taking one for the team. My first band experience was formed.

Finding Inspiration

I found some inspiration when I heard a friend of one of my older brothers, who was messing around with playing bass, built two bass cabinets himself and created his own bass rig. I thought this was so cool and somehow, I was able to listen to him play his bass through his super loud bass rig. I was blown away by the loudness of this bass rig and the feeling of bass notes pounding through my chest. I'll never forget that feeling -it was like thunder! I thought to myself that if bass was going to be like that then I might actually want to be a bass player. I just couldn't believe that bass could be like that.

Then I started to think that maybe I should buy a bass because I was trying to play bass on a guitar. I started looking at what bass and amp I should buy. I saw bass players in *Hit Parader* magazine like Chris Squire and Geddy Lee playing a Rickenbacher bass. I thought that was the coolest bass ever, so I started to try and find a music store that sold one. The music store I took lessons at didn't carry that kind of bass. Then someone told me about this big music store in Flint off Dort Hwy, I think it was called Flint Music. I walked in there and I saw this sienna burst Rickenbacher copy made by Kay. I fell in love with this bass and begged my dad to buy it for me. It took him a little bit to come around to the idea and eventually he was gracious enough to buy it, and that was my first bass guitar.

Little did he know what he was doing for me that day. For me, it was the beginning of a love for bass guitar. I am so thankful for that day. We had to have an amp as well, so we found a used one in the classified ads of the paper - it was a 60-watt Marlboro amp- yes Marlboro I guess made amps as well. We then went to the guy's house and bought that amp and brought it home. I remember plugging in that Kay sienna burst Rickenbacher copy and jamming out as loud as I could push that amp. I was hooked on bass guitar now and wanted to learn everything I could to get better at it.

I ended up having my guitar teacher start teaching me bass. He told me that he could only take me so far then I would have to find a different teacher. I was good with that and so after 6 months of lessons I learned many blues and pentatonic scales which would set the tone for my style of playing. It really lent itself to classic rock and 80's hair band music. The sound that was created with these scales and the music I was listening to was developing my thinking as a bass player.

First Studio Experience

During this time, the rhythm guitar player of our neighborhood band, Craig, was actually writing songs. This was amazing! Now I had a chance to write bass lines and create grooves using the knowledge I received from bass lessons. We all had no idea what we were doing and what it meant that we were writing songs at the age of 12 and 13.

Then Craig pulled us together to rehearse so we could go into the studio. His guitar teacher had connections to a studio in Flint. We decided on 3 songs: "Alloy States," "I Need You," and "Power To Rock." "Alloy States" was my first song where I learned how to drive eighth notes and then accent hits with the drummer. I thought I was the best bass player in the world. The song "I Need You" was a good rocking song as well. The song "Power to Rock" was one I was very proud of because it was my first time creating walking bass lines, and I had a bass solo in it. A solo where the band stops, and I say something on my bass. I loved playing these songs in Craig's basement.

I really started to invest myself into playing bass, writing these songs and recording in the studio. I started to develop a love for bass at this point. It was also the beginning of me gaining confidence that I could play bass and actually create a bass line in my head and then put it into the instrument of bass. This is an accomplishment I am very proud of as a bass player. I still have those recordings 40 years later.

Discovering My Two Biggest Influences

Right after this studio experience, I was listening to a lot of different bands. Then I came across the song “Ramble On” by Led Zeppelin and it changed my bass playing forever. When I heard John Paul Jones playing on that song I was blown away. It had a soothing melody, rock punch and upbeat notes perfectly placed. It showed me that bass was more than playing the same thing as the guitar player or driving quarter notes underneath cool guitar riffs all the time. Bass could actually be an interesting instrument and contribute something cool. John Paul Jones was my first major influence of how to play bass and write bass lines. Being self-taught I ended up studying John Paul Jones' style and tried to model my playing after his.

What I learned from John Paul Jones was to make my bass lines more syncopated and percussive. Because of that I started to develop a special technique with my right hand, and a combination of ghost notes and chokes with my left hand. This would lend itself to fill out the sound of a band. I was very excited to develop this technique and I realized that by applying it I could hold my own if there was no other instrument playing. This was a big deal to me. I didn't want to depend on a drummer to make me sound good. I would practice the bass lines until they sounded good on their own with nothing else. This became my goal and practice habit. Craig was already writing new songs so it was awesome that I would have the opportunity to develop and apply this approach and style of bass playing. I use this approach to this day, and it is something I am very proud of.

Another bass player worth mentioning was Steve Harris from Iron Maiden. I was really into Iron Maiden at the age of 13, and they came out with an album called *Number of the Beast*. This whole album was awesome, especially the bass playing of Steve Harris. The title track "Number of the Beast" really stood out for his bass work. That bass line specifically gave me another approach to bass. It challenged me to see bass as a melodicallydriven instrument, and how the bass creates direction for the song. It taught me that bass as an instrument can lead a song and move it forward like pioneering a path, and bringing the rest of the band with it. This album was a game changer for me all the way around as I was developing as a bass player.

Steve Harris's bass work also challenged me to start learning my scales. Being self-taught in the 1980s was a little different than being in the internet age. By the time I was 15 I had developed my ear and was figuring out what sounded good. I learned that melody is structured and there is a reason why some notes sound better than others. His bass lines helped me understand this. It wasn't just random notes. There would seem to be several melodic bass solos throughout this album but that was just his style. I was able to pull from his style and started learning how to be melodic with my bass lines.

Becoming My Own

Two members moved on, so it became just guitar, bass and drums. Now, we were a power trio. Craig ended up writing some very complicated guitar parts and Jack was an incredible drummer. As a bass player I had to step up and write bass lines that measured up to their talent. This was a great opportunity to apply what

I was learning from John Paul Jones and Steve Harris.

I played with a pick as a bass player instead of my fingers. I didn't really get that fat sound because of that, but I was able to develop a sound and style that was unique. I was able to understand what I call 'ghost notes', and how to take a riff and make it more rhythmic and sound like it's going somewhere. I didn't know any better, it just made sense to do this. I developed a style of bass playing, in that if the drums and other instruments disappeared, my bass line would hold its own by itself. This was important for me to be able to do. I did not want to be dependent on any other band member to make me sound good. Playing with a pick allowed me to fill out the bass line with a lot of syncopation and create forward direction in the song.

It was an exciting time for me because I felt like I was finally getting good at something. We would spend a lot of time arranging and figuring out how to make these songs we were writing interesting. Dissecting the songs right down to the last hi-hat hit or the last bass choke or Craig's choice of chord color for the songs. It was an amazing time in my life. Three years from the age of 13 to 16, I was in the trenches of writing bass-lines and developing my technique and style of playing. It was during this time that my bass identity would blossom.

Although every song was unique and had

its own character, there were 4 songs in particular that defined my style, even to this day. There was the 10-minute song "In The Dark," "Song X," "Cops and Robbers" and a no title song in D Mixolydian. These songs challenged me to play my bass from bottom to top of the bass neck, with upbeats and chokes, melody and drive, with groove and solos. It challenged me to step into a realm of bass playing I never thought possible. It was like the proving grounds for me to learn, the battlefield for me to earn my stripes. We would end up recording all these songs throughout high school.

During this time, I gained confidence and felt like I had a purpose, with value and worth. My purpose was being a bass player- I felt like I existed to play bass. My value was what I contributed to this power trio- I had something to offer. My worth was something I really thought I deserved because of my hard work and dedication to this music, and I deserved to be recognized as a superior bass player. You see where this is going don't you? I started to become very arrogant to say the least.

There was no competition in the area, and I wanted recognition for my accomplishment on bass. I would really take any compliments from anyone who wanted to hand them out. As I got older, I realized that bass was something that made sense to me and came easy for me to play and create and compose on. It was something that

I could say that 'I' did with no help from anyone else, only 'I' figured out how to play the bass. You could say I took pride in what I accomplished but that led to a stench of arrogance. There was a type of self-actualization that happened because I felt there was a fulfillment of my talents and potentialities. I was around 16 when this started to happen, and it would be the beginning of extreme arrogance in my life.

Craig and Jack graduated high school the year before me, so they kinda moved on. We tried to do one last studio session for a song that Craig was working on before we split but, the enthusiasm was lost for all of us to keep going. Craig ended up moving to Florida and Jack ended up moving out of the Flushing area. I was jamming with these two guys for about 8 years. We created a lot of awesome music, and it was a time in my life that I will never forget. It is where I grew up musically and developed a passion for music and studio recording. It was also where I learned how to be a bass player and allow my mind to be creative. To Craig and Jack- thank you for the good times.

Joining Surreal

While in high school I became good friends with 2 classmates, Scott and Ben. Scott was an aspiring vocalist and Ben picked up the guitar while in High School. Scott actually cut some vocal tracks over the music we wrote in Craigs basement. He took on the challenge of writing lyrics and melody over that crazy music. I have to say he did a good job coming up with something considering the music wasn't really designed for vocals. We just realized that we were a power trio and vocals were not in the song's DNA.

Ben would come over and hang out in Craig's basement while we rehearsed. This was pretty cool because we developed a friendship. Even though he told me I was an arrogant person when I played bass, I still thought he was a pretty cool guy. He picked up the guitar when he was 17 and really took to it.

I remember when my power trio was together Ben accepted a challenge of learning Craig's guitar lines for a gig we were doing. Now remember, Craig's guitar lines were not normal. They were very complicated and unorthodox- in a good way. We all thought there was no way Ben could learn those songs in such a short time. Well, he did learn those guitar lines. In fact, he learned them good enough to do the gig. Much respect for him when he did that.

Scott and Ben ended up forming the band Surreal. I already had a friendship with both of them so after Craig and Jack moved on, I ended up joining the band Surreal. They had some real good music when I joined the band. We started to make plans to write some new music and go into the studio to record an album.

Nickname

After I joined Surreal, I also started college at Mott Community College as a music major. As I made new friends in college, we would find ways to hang out and get to know each other and have some fun. One day during my first semester of my freshman year, some classmates and I went to an iconic coney island restaurant in Flint called Angelos, off Franklin Avenue. Super-greasy food, but it was so delicious and at that time I really didn't care.

Anyway, I had a reputation of being able to eat a lot of food in one setting. The expression back then was 'let's go mow' which meant let's go eat. When the four of us were done they wanted to take my picture at the booth with all the empty plates and napkins looking like I am the one who ate, or mowed, all that food. There was a sign on the wall at each booth that said, 'Reserved For 4 or More'. Well, this one was a bit worn, so it only read 'Reserved For 4 or Mo' since the 're' was broken off the sign. That's why my friends wanted to take a picture of me in the booth because I 'mowed' all that food.

Ever since that day, the nickname 'Mo' has stuck with me. In light of that, I started letting everyone know that my stage name would be Mo

Jones and not Mike Jones. Some people to this day still think my real name is Mo Jones.

God's Plan Begins

"Many are the plans in the mind of a man, but it is the purpose of the Lord that will stand." Proverbs 19:21 ESV

Growing up musically I had no idea what God would do with my love for bass and music. God has a plan for everyone and that includes me. As I look back, it is obvious that He was grooming me to be a bass player/musician for His plan and purpose for my life. Even though I didn't think "Hey, I think I'm going to learn bass for Jesus," He was still grooming me. I really had no intent of playing bass for Jesus. As a young boy I wanted to rock the stage and travel the world. I didn't want to play bass for Jesus, I didn't even know who Jesus was really. I wanted to tour the world with loud music and be a rockstar. **Even at a young age the Holy Spirit was dropping seeds in me to create a desire to have a love for music and more specifically the bass.** I really didn't want to play the bass at first but over time my desire for any other instrument like guitar or piano went to the back burner and bass came to the forefront. Like I said, the bass guitar just came easy for me and it felt natural. Like I was meant to play bass.

Experiencing God's Will

Everyone seems to have this idea that God has to be dramatic and make it known what He is doing. It was not obvious that the Holy Spirit was working on me. As a matter of fact I was oblivious to the situation. But there were two experiences which stuck out as huge seeds to create that desire for bass and music.

The first one was when He (Holy Spirit) allowed me to hear my brother's friend's bass rig. The one where I thought '*If this is bass then I am in.*' This was a massive rig with pounding bass. But this tangible, physical experience gave me a vision for what bass does. As the bass notes pounded in my body, I thought, "Now that was some bass!" I loved, and still do to this day, the feeling of bass being the loud booming foundation and shaking the walls.

The second experience was when the Holy Spirit allowed me to hear the song "Ramble On" by Led Zeppelin. I was stunned when I heard it the first time. This song showed me what bass is capable of in the sense of being able to be soft for one moment and then go to a pounding low end groove at the drop of a hat. In other words, it showed me that it can be a very dynamic instrument.

These 2 experiences were instrumental in cementing the idea that I wanted to be a bass player for life. It took me from the attitude of *'I'll take one for the team'* to *'I desire to be a bass player'*. This was important because it gave me vision and focus. My desire for any other instrument went away. God knows what He is doing.

God will do what He wants, when He wants and how He wants to bring about His purpose. He could have chosen an on-fire Christian to come into my life and mentor me on bass or use a Christian rock song. Instead, He used what was around me to accomplish His will. My brother's friend was not an on-fire Christian. Maybe he was saved, I don't know, but either way the Holy Spirit still used him for His purpose. Led Zeppelin was not a Christian rock band. As a matter of fact, some of their songs have been criticized for being Satanic. Yet, the Holy Spirit still used that song "Ramble On" to bring about His purpose for my life.

This would be the beginning of me identifying as a bass player. I would soon find out that a bass player is who I was meant to be. But it had to start somewhere. The Holy Spirit planted the seed and these experiences allowed the seed to take root, and my identity as a bass player was birthed. Time would allow this identity to take root deeper and grow. Remember this: **Whatever seed takes root in you will start to develop**

an identity, whether it's good or bad. In this instance, it was good.

Teaching Me Bass

The Holy Spirit would continue to stir up my desire to learn and come up with ideas of how to be a bass player. You could say that the Holy Spirit was my best bass teacher, in a way. When I played bass, it just made sense what I should do to make it sound good. How to hold it and how to approach it. I would listen to music that I liked, and then try and emulate what I heard bass-wise.

For example, my left-hand technique came to me out of the blue. I didn't have any teacher telling me how to hold my neck. I didn't have any teacher tell me how to use a pick or my fingers while playing bass, it just came to me. I don't know where it came from... ahh wait yes, I do, the Holy Spirit. *'Now Mike you are crazy saying that the Holy Spirit taught you bass.'* Well, that's a different debate, I suppose. All I know is everything I taught myself was by the book even though I didn't have a book to go by. Again, God can do what He wants, when he wants, and how He wants. Even if I wasn't saved.

Is it possible for the Holy Spirit to work in a situation where Jesus is not Lord of someone's life? The answer is yes, He can. The Holy Spirit works in the midst of any situation with any person to bring about God's will. God's will is that all are saved and come to a knowledge of the truth. But before one comes to a knowledge of the truth, the Holy Spirit is at work making that opportunity happen. We will talk about that later.

Was I saved while He, the Holy Spirit, was inspiring me to be a bass player? The answer is no, I was not saved. He was developing me to be a bass player for the Lord Almighty without me even knowing it. God had a plan. And in His sovereignty, He was making His plan come to pass. He planted the seed, and it took root. I was developing this love for bass and music. Even though my motives were not lined up with God's motives, the Holy Spirit was right there making sure I was staying engaged with the bass.

Arrogance

Now to everything good, there is always an adversary. One who wants to see you fail and be miserable. Along the way of building a desire to be a bass player, other seeds were being sown and I was developing a stench of arrogance. These seeds would come from God's adversary...you got it, Satan or the devil. I mean, the name Satan means 'adversary', or 'one opposed to.' Some people told me that the devil doesn't exist and there was no reason to get worked up. Some even said I was overreacting.

In my own eyes I really thought I was something. I really felt like I was on top of the bass world, and I could do anything bass-wise put in front of me. Unfortunately, I would let everyone know that I thought I was the bomb on bass when I performed. I used to do this weird awkward head-bob thing when I would play, and I was told by friends that I would come across as arrogant when I did that head-bob thing. Then I would say "I can't help it that I am awesome on bass." Yeah, I was full of myself for sure. The Bible says *"As it is, you boast in your arrogance. All such boasting is evil."*James 4:16 ESV

I didn't know any better though, because I was ignorant of understanding God's Word. I mean when I blossomed as a bass player It made me feel like I was good at something. The comments and compliments from other people made me feel like I was something special. I felt accepted and that my skills on bass demanded the respect from others even if they were not my friend. It's almost like it gave me this stamp of approval from my family and friends, and even those who were not friends with me.

Even though the Holy Spirit was planting a seed for God's purpose, without me even realizing it, the devil was right there planting seeds of arrogance, without me realizing it. You could say that the kingdom of Satan was hard at work trying to destroy the work of what the Holy Spirit was doing. **Arrogance is like yeast- it can work**

through the whole batch of dough and destroy it. *"Your boasting is not good. Do you not know that a little leaven leavens the whole lump?"* 1 Corinthians 5:6 ESV

But nonetheless, identifying as a bass player was becoming well-established within myself. Even with the arrogance taking root as well, it couldn't destroy my identity developing as a bass player. At that time, I still had no clue what was going on, but God in His sovereignty had a plan and purpose for my life, even if I wasn't acknowledging Him as the Lord of my life. Glory to God for He is Sovereign! His plans and purpose will always be established!!

CHAPTER 2
"START OUT YOUNG"

Spiritual Identity - The Soul - Seeds

1976- Summer 1983

Stirred Up! Star Wars

Television and movies were the first thing to start developing my spiritual identity. Everything that I watched as a young boy was based around the idea that evil will try to win over good, and even though it seems like evil will prevail, good always finds a way to claim victory. Sound familiar? That's just what makes up good TV and movies. Some of the classics like Cinderella, Wizard of Oz, It's A Wonderful Life. The story line of so many movies were, and still are, evil or a bad situations that are overcome by good and we all live happily ever after.

When I was 7 years old the movie *Star Wars* came out and I just thought that movie was the bomb. I connected with all the characters in that movie. Luke Skywalker and the gang represented good and Darth Vader and his stormtroopers represented evil and they are in the midst of an ongoing war. You all know the story! I watched that movie and bought a lot of the merchandise that came out afterwards and even played the characters out with friends, re-enacting the movie. I mean in the 1970's we were all over this movie and everyone loved it. With that said to this day it's one of the best representations of good vs evil in a movie. Actually, the next two *Empire strikes Back* and *Return of the Jedi* were just as good representing good vs evil. Every kid was into this idea of good guys vs bad guys, right?

The most interesting thing in these movies was the reliance on faith that the rebels, the Jedi's especially, had in 'The Force'. This Force became sort of the central point of the movie to me. My little mind was trying to figure this out, how could something unseen have such a big influence on human life. This blew my mind for a long time. The idea that I can't see it but somehow, I can connect to it. I started to wonder if that was something that could happen to me. Maybe there was some kind of 'Force' that I could tap into. Even Darth Vader was influenced by some other 'force', that being the dark side.

As a young boy I would ask myself "Is this something that is a reality in the real world?" I would also ask, "is there such a thing as a 'good' that is unseen that fights against evil?" I think as kids we have all had similar experiences one way or another. For me, this was the beginning of trying to figure out this concept of good vs evil in the real world. Just so I am clear, these Star Wars movies are not bad for causing me to ponder this. They just started the ball rolling for me to try and understand good vs evil in the real world. This concept I was trying to understand would be the beginning of things to come.

Kiss- First Demonic Thoughts

About the same time *Star Wars* came out I was introduced to my first musical influence. The rock band KISS. They were emerging in the mid 1970's and I was really loving their music. I became a huge KISS fan. Their album *KISS Alive* was my favorite album, probably because I really was not exposed to any other bands other than my parents' country music. I can't remember who had the album for me to listen to. I think it was either my brother or my friend Craig. Somehow, I got a hold of that album, and I would listen to this album over and over.

I really loved the costumes and make-up the band members put on for their image. It was fun trying to figure out what each member's costume was, but Gene Simmons was the most intriguing one for me. He dressed as a demon. There were pictures of him blowing fire out of his mouth inside the album artwork, which I thought was very cool. There were also pictures of one of his other gimmicks in which blood would start oozing out of his mouth and cover his face. I mean, he looked and acted like an actual demon.

So why was I so into Gene Simmons? I don't know, I just loved his whole gimmick. As a young kid I didn't understand it was a gimmick, but it really put a lot of thoughts in my head about what darkness could be. I mean there was fire, blood and leather wings to boot. And for some reason I wanted to try and understand this representation of a demon. So now I was on a journey to find out more about demons.

The Exorcist

As I was wanting to know more about demons, I had heard about a movie that came out in 1973 called *The Exorcist*. I became obsessed with wanting to watch it. When I was 10 years old, and I begged my parents to let me watch this movie. My parents told me that I would have nightmares after seeing it, but I didn't care, I just wanted to see it so bad. They eventually gave in and rented the VHS and let me watch it one night. It scared the crap out of me, and sure enough, I could not sleep for several nights. My parents were right in not wanting me to see this movie.

I think what terrified me about that movie was the fact that there were real humans dealing with something that could actually happen in real life. Star Wars was made up, but *The Exorcist* was a reality and possible. I couldn't believe how much control evil (the demons in Linda Blair) had over good (the priests). Good could not just waltz into the room where the possessed person was and zap them to make everything better. The portrayal of those demons in Linda Blair was amazingly real, and as a 10-year-old, it freaked me out. Now you would think that I would not want anything to do with the dark side after that movie. On the contrary, I actually wanted to know more. I really had no idea where this push to know the dark side was coming from.

That is my first recollection of me starting to understand that there is a battle of good and evil, angels and demons. It started to take root in my mind as I was sorting this out. Then I started thinking about whether there were demons around me or not. At first it freaked me out, but after the initial shock of watching that movie, it eventually became no big deal. It was like I was becoming more comfortable with the dark side.

Even though I was interested in the dark side after watching that movie, I thought maybe

I would want to be a priest. Yes, the dark side was drawing me in, but there was something else that was drawing me to want to go against the demons like the priest in *The Exorcist*. When I saw those priests reading the Word of God in that movie, I was really moved by the conviction they had when they read it. Those Bible readings in the movie seemed to have a sense of power when it was spoken over the demon-possessed girl in the movie. There was purpose in what they were doing. All of this was causing me to fixate on what is going on in the spirit realm around me. I felt like there was a war over me, like two promptings inside me, each presenting their case to follow them.

The Music (1980- Summer 1983)

So right after I experienced the movie, *The Exorcist*, the music of that day stepped up to take over shaping my spiritual identity. Like I said the first band that I connected with was KISS but then, in 1980 I was introduced to the band AC/DC. They would have a huge influence on me as a young 10-year-old boy. When their album *Back In Black* came out, I was like "wow" I have to get this album. I loved the sound of their guitar and the rhythm section. One song in particular was "Rock n Roll Ain't Noise Pollution." This song had soul in the guitar and vocals and the bass line was very interesting. All my music sensors were on high alert as I took a liking to this band and that song.

I remember as a kid I would crank this song up when it came on the radio. I found out what the album title was, so I made plans to go and buy it. Now back in my day buying an album was a big deal. It was like a cool experience to go out and buy one. The album store I went to was Grapevine Records over on Clio Rd in Flint. For my birthday that year I got just enough money to buy the album, so I went and got it. I remember walking into that store, the excitement, and the smell of the cellophane wrapped around the album. It was quite the experience.

I was so excited to bring this album home. I had this little blue record player in my room with two speakers hooked to it. I put that album on that record player and carefully dropped the needle down on the vinyl album and then cranked it up and jammed it out. I'll never forget that feeling I had when that music connected with me. It was like someone introduced me to a new friend in a way. All I could do now is chase the feeling this music brought to me. I became a huge fan of AC/DC and I wore that album out! I really didn't understand the meaning of the lyrics. I just knew that I liked the sound of the band and the drive behind the music.

After listening to this album I remember having, I'll call it, a *memorable moment* in my life. I had a conversation with myself about whether I was going to continue with hard rock music like AC/DC or keep listening to country music like my parents. My parents would always play country music everywhere we went. Our drives up north, vacations, even trips to the grocery store. My dad loved country music and he also loved cranking it up in the car when we went somewhere. I thought that was so cool.

I didn't dislike the country music but just didn't connect with it. So anyway, I'm talking to myself like there are two people presenting both styles of music. I went back and forth for a few weeks as each voice was working hard to persuade me. One voice would say that "country music was more mellow and adult like", while the other voice would say that "rock is more fun and everyone your age listens to rock". This became a very stressful decision for me at 10 years old. I really needed to resolve this inside of myself.

Then one day I was alone in my room and the voices became really intense almost like they were arguing with one another. Then it happened. I remember being convinced of what I wanted to do. I made a decision to become a rocker. I would shout, "I am a rocker!" several times as I was in my bedroom sitting on the floor holding onto my Back in Black album. It was like I was making a commitment to this style of music. Like a covenant or something. I remember a feeling of rebellion coming over me and a strange laugh came out of my mouth. I thought to myself *'What was that?'* then I blew it off and jammed out to AC/DC.

As time went on, I wanted to explore other songs from AC/DC, so I started checking out their older albums. I came across their song "Highway to Hell," which was the title track to their album before *Back In Black*. I thought this song was the greatest song ever written. Eventually, I bought that album, and "*Highway to Hell*" became my new favorite song and album. I would listen to that album from start to finish over and over, especially the song "Highway to Hell," which became like an anthem in my 11 years of life. I would sing the chorus over and over and over...

I'm on the highway to hell
On the highway to hell
Highway to hell
I'm on the highway to hell

Then I started paying attention to what the verses had to say. The first verse made reference that it was a big party, and one would see their friends in hell having a good time. Painting the picture that hell was one big party in the afterlife. Then the next verse refers to Hell as being the promised land. Like a land where you could do whatever you wanted and live it up. I would raise my glass of pop and say to friends I'm on the highway to hell and laugh about it. I didn't know what I was saying, you could say that I was just ignorant. I didn't know any better.

This one song would have a huge influence on me and become foundational for developing my spiritual identity whether it be good or bad. I started to agree with what this song said in the lyrics as I sang it more and more. I would even write the lyrics out by memory while I was in school. In a way, it was like those verses were a sermon of sorts and then the confession of faith that I was on a path to hell. As I repeated those lyrics in ignorance, I was building a foundation for my soul to have reason to rebel against all that I knew was good and right.

Heaven And Hell

The idea of good vs evil, heaven vs hell was at full tilt in my brain and the fire of this new sound of music was influencing me. I heard the song "Heaven and Hell" by Black Sabbath, and it became the next important song to influence me for my spiritual development. This song, like almost every song from that era, had lyrics that were very ambiguous and open to interpretation. The chorus of the song was what I heard though. Like the other songs, I would sing the chorus over and over.

Ronnie James Dio, the guy who wrote this song, stated that, "The song is about the ability of each human being to choose between doing good and doing evil. Essentially that each person has heaven and hell inside themselves." This song started gluing together the idea that heaven = doing good, and hell = doing bad. I saw this song as I had a choice to do good or evil. Like there was a battle in the unseen world for me to do one or the other. In my head, I started to believe that there had to be a battle going on all the time around us. I didn't really understand this battle but, in my mind, this just made sense that there was a battle of good and evil.

My favorite lyric in that song is "*And they'll tell you black is really white / The moon is just the sun at night / It's heaven and hell.*" My mind was just trying to figure this out. It put in me that there is a stark difference between the two. It's like they are opposite but coexist and fight for dominance over the other. Like a battle. I would always be wondering if this battle of demons and angels, good and evil, heaven and hell was even real. I thought to myself that it had to be real, but I still had doubts. This would be added to the fixation of this concept. It was like something inside me was putting this on the forefront of my thinking.

This song "Heaven and Hell" has some of the greatest music ever written. The bass line was very influential, and I loved the soaring guitar melodies. I really liked the scale choice and chord choice they used in this song. In combination of the lyrics and the music I felt like I could make a spiritual connection to this song. I'm not sure how to say it other than I felt like this song was in my soul. When I listened to this song it took me on a spiritual journey. This song would set the tone for my future song writing style and it introduced me to the idea of classical type melody.

The Number Of The Beast

After I wore that album out, I was turned on to the band Iron Maiden. This is where things started to get interesting for me. In 1982, when I was 13, I picked up their album *Number of the Beast* and it quickly became my new favorite album. Every song on the album was great but the title track "Number of the Beast" became my, you guessed it, new favorite song. The song started out with Vincent Price speaking Scripture from the Book of Revelation - I just thought that was the coolest thing ever.

Woe to you, oh Earth and sea, for the Devil sends the Beast with wrath

Because he knows the time is short

Let him who hath understanding reckon the number of the Beast

For it is a human number, its number is six hundred, and sixty-six.

This opening dialogue was something that

you could say echoed within me. It was like I couldn't stop thinking about this idea of 666 being the number of the beast. I mean what was this number and why 666? A friend of mine told me that dialogue came from the book of Revelation in the Bible. That was interesting to me because in my mind it lined up with this whole idea of heaven and hell, good versus evil concept, and now it added God versus the devil into the mystery. Well, in my mind it was a mystery. I interpreted the intro as a calling on evil to destroy what is good because you don't have much time. In other words: Go to war.

Another friend of mine turned me onto this article in the magazine *Hit Parader* that talked about the making of this album. The article talked about strange things that happened at the studio as they recorded it. One incident that stuck out is when the producer, Martin Birch, was in a car accident, and the bill came to 666 pounds. Was that a coincidence? I am not sure why, but I thought that was so cool that the bill came to 666 pounds. In my mind it was confirming more to me that the dark side was real.

When the music of "The Number of the Beast" kicks in and Bruce Dickenson starts singing, the meaning of the song starts to come to life. The Vincent Price intro had a different meaning than what the song was actually written about. I interpreted the song to be about a person who starts to see dark shadows and questions as to whether or not they are real. By the end of the song the person is overcome by these spirits of darkness. As I saw interviews with Steve Harris later in life, that's not too far off from how he explained what the song was about.

"Heaven and Hell" caused me to think about the overall battle, but this song "Number of the Beast" drew me into a conversation within myself. It was a conversation as to whether individual dark spirits were real and how they can lure you in until they have full control. The more and more I listened to that song the more I thought about the spirit realm and how darkness overcame good. Maybe it was my mind playing tricks on me, but I thought I started to see shadows out of the corner of my eye.

This was a hard concept to grasp. How could darkness win at anything? I have been programmed to think that good wins no matter what. The darkness does have some wins within the battle but in the end good overcomes and wins. But this song "Number of the Beast" darkness wins. Darkness overcomes the person and takes full control. I've never thought about this before, and I started to wonder what it would be like if darkness would take control of me. It was a strange thing to think about but for some reason that desire was developing within me.

See You In Hell

There is one more band and song I think worth mentioning because it was the one that pushed me over the edge to start pursuing the things of the dark side. The band was Grim Reaper with the song "See You In Hell." Yes, another song about hell. Seems like there were a lot of songs about hell back then. If "Highway to Hell" was an invitation for me to get on the path to hell, and "Number Of The Beast" was a realization that the dark side does exist and they will eventually take over my being, then the song "See You In Hell" was a proclamation of my final destination after I die.

Seems like all the lyrics in the song were "*see you in hell my friend*" sung over and over. Again, like every other song I would scream this chorus from the top of my lungs, and it became like another anthem for me. It was like something was programming my mind to believe I was destined to go to hell after I died. There were times when I would get done listening to that song, screaming it at the top of my lungs, and I would just feel different. Like I was arrogantly untouchable, or something like I had a touch from the dark side.

Music Influences

"The heart is deceitful above all things, and desperately sick; who can understand it?"
Jeremiah 17:9 ESV

All of this music was influencing me right along as I was developing as a bass player. There was a lot of music in the early to mid-1980's that lyrically talked about hell, one way or another. It was a hot topic I guess you could say, and it seemed like all of those songs were finding their way to me. There were others I did not mention like Van Halen's "Runnin With The Devil," Dio's "Holy Diver," and more - but the ones I shared were the most influential.

The experience of committing to being a rocker was a spiritual battle for me. Even leading up to that day, there was a tossing back and forth within two different arguments of which would be best suited for me. It wasn't other voices, it was my own voice in my own head reasoning with myself about whether to be a rocker.

There were two sides at work putting certain desires within me to consider. I'm going to say that it wasn't God who was putting the desire in me to want to be a rocker, so therefore, it had to be of the devil. There's nothing in between. I don't think it's the rock music sound that God didn't like, it was the lyrics and what they promoted- which was Satan and his kingdom.

It was a memorable experience as I recall the inner voice changing that day to something like a different person. The voice took on a personality and started to pressure me to commit to being a rocker. I remember I was getting ready to do it and it was like jumping off a diving board for the first time. I was like 'alright here I go…' and then I would stop. I would do that a few times. Then it was like the voice somehow comforted me to believe I could do this. I got the nerve up and just blurted it out...off the diving board I went. I dove into that pool to be a rocker.

What was that voice? Was it a voice of reason inside me? Maybe it was a demon? *'Oh no Mike it couldn't be a demon.'* Hmm, I wonder why someone would say that it couldn't be a demon. I believe it is very possible that it was a demon that brought me to that commitment. You could say that Satan got a win that day. Of course, God let him win but that's a different discussion.

Let me explain why I think it was more than likely a demon. When those words came off my lips "I am a rocker!!" something changed inside of me, and it made me feel different. I was grinning and feeling more aggressive in my attitude, and why was there strange laughs coming out of me while holding on to that AC/DC album? There was a celebration in my head like there were others telling me it was the right choice. Who knows, maybe there were many demons…

As I look back, I believe I was making an agreement with something dark. What I experienced was not of God during this moment. It had to be of Satan. **Remember if it's not of God then it is of Satan.** There is nothing in-between, it's one or the other - no gray areas. Besides what came after this 'commitment to be a rocker' proves my point.

Satan influenced my mind to be a part of something that was against God by introducing me to music like AC/DC's "Highway to Hell." That was the start of a tirade of music that was all about Satan and demons. Call me crazy but go back and look at the titles of the songs that conveniently became my favorite songs. Do you think maybe these songs influenced me just a little bit: "Highway to Hell," "Heaven and Hell," "666 The Number of the Beast," "See You In Hell?"

'You are a wack job Mike; those songs were harmless.' Harmless, eh? I challenge you to find me someone who can listen to those songs and honestly confess Jesus as their Lord. Anyone who is a true believer want to try that? Go ahead... I'm waiting. If anyone is a true believer, you will not be able to sing those songs about Satan and his kingdom. Those songs are a confession of the complete opposite of who Christ Jesus is and what He did for us by dying on the cross, saving us from the patterns of this world and taking away our sin. You cannot confess *'I am on the highway to hell'* and then confess *'Jesus is my Lord.'* Prove me wrong...Anyone??

If you really understand what Jesus has done for you and me, there is no way that you can let each of those word phrases come out of your mouth. *"From the same mouth come blessing and cursing. My brothers, these things ought not to be so. Does a spring pour forth from the same opening both fresh and salt water? Can a fig tree, my brothers, bear olives, or a grapevine produce figs? Neither can a salt pond yield fresh water."* James 3:10-12 ESV

But growing up I would sing the salty lyrics that were not the things of God. For whatever reason I desired those lyrics above anything else. It was a curse to sing those songs. Jesus even teaches us that out of the abundance of the heart the mouth speaks. The Bible says *"Either make the tree good and its fruit good, or make the tree bad and its fruit bad, for the tree is known by its fruit. You brood of vipers! How can you speak good, when you are evil? For out of the abundance of the heart the mouth speaks."* Matthew 12:33-37 ESV

The Heart

The heart is the battlefield in which Satan and the Word of God interact. Satan cannot stop or stand against the Word of God. Satan can only accuse you and try and influence you to do something. He cannot make you do anything, but he can create desire within you, so you want to do things that contradict God's Word.

'Our hearts are prone to wander' the old hymn "Come Thou Fount of Every Blessing" says, and this is a true statement. Our hearts are prone to wander when the Word of God is not rooted and established within the soil of our heart. We are dead in our sin *"And you were dead in the trespasses and sins,"* Ephesians 2:1 ESV

So even as a young boy, the devil was hard at work trying to form my heart to be rebellious towards God. I was so young and didn't know any better and the devil knew that, and this made me easy prey. The devil kept this kind of music in front of me, where I didn't want any other kind of music. Out of ignorance I thought this music was what I needed and wanted. Now call me a judgmental conservative who is freaking out about adolescent music if you want - but I lived it growing up.

Why did it affect me differently than some of my friends? I'm not too sure, all I can say is I was in deep with this kind of music, and it affected my being in a very negative way. It consumed my mind while forming my thoughts and worldview. Music makes a difference and can have tremendous influence on us. Young or old, male or female it doesn't matter.

In the mid-1990's, I ended up leading a Bible study at my church for the youth, about 15 kids. I was talking to them about this very topic of how music will influence you. I did an experiment and had them all sit in the room and relax and just talk and hang out. After 10 minutes of them doing this, I then played some hard rock music for about 15 minutes and told them to keep talking and hanging out. I then stopped the music, and we had a conversation about how this music made them feel. Did it change the thoughts going through their minds at the time the hard rock music was being played?

This led to a vibrant conversation of how music changes the mood and thoughts of people. Some of the kids admitted that they felt looser and more open to things that were not of God. Like drinking, lying, and just doing things that were of-the-flesh. One youth even said they felt like smoking a joint- I'm not exaggerating.

There was one youth who talked to me privately about his home situation and how he felt oppressed all the time. He was 16 and wanted so badly to have a relationship with his parents. They seemed to be rejecting him. I felt led by the Spirit to talk to him about the music that he listens to. Come to find out he was a huge fan of bands that were of the alternative metal- shock metal of the early to mid 1990's. Some of these bands had lyrics that were outright anti-God and destructive. I took a chance and told him to give up that kind of music and I would intercede for him as well.

About a week goes by and it was just amazing the change that happened in this young man. He was smiling and optimistic and just had a great outlook on life, which was the complete opposite of how he was when I met him. He told me that since he stopped listening to that genre of music, his life has been different. I was so happy to hear that. Then about 4 weeks later he stopped coming to the youth group. I was concerned of course and then I finally saw him, and he admitted that he went back to listening to that genre of music. He said he couldn't help himself.

Of course, I was bummed out and did everything I could to get him back in the youth group. But all of my efforts didn't bring him back. I believe this was a spiritual battle going on and Satan was using this genre of music to keep this youth oppressed and in a state of mind that was destructive. My heart was broken.

I could definitely relate to what he was dealing with, because of my own experience. That time in my life was the beginning of Satan using music to oppress me, forming my thoughts and worldview. Music is so powerful to influence in a good way or in a negative way. There is an example of music influencing a situation in the Bible when David was the house musician for king Saul.

"David would take up his lyre and play. Then relief would come to Saul; he would feel better, and the evil spirit would leave him.'

1 Samuel 16:23 ESV

When you read this passage of scripture there is no denying that music moved spirits in the spirit realm. It says that a tormenting spirit came on Saul and David would play and Saul would get relief and the spirit would leave him. With music having that kind of powerful effect on Saul to drive away a tormenting spirit, what do you think would happen if you play the type of music that is in the demon's wheelhouse? You know, confessing who Satan is and saying that you are on 'the highway to hell' and confessing to people 'see you in hell' (song from Grim Reaper). I'll tell you what will happen based on my experience- It confuses you and deceives you to think that God is not all-powerful and is not your friend. It affects your being.

Music was the main tool Satan used to corrupt my heart at a young age. As I internalized the songs, I allowed them to mold my way of thinking and my world views. The lyrics and repeating the choruses over and over and over of those songs would be the strongest influence. Naturally the heart is wicked anyway, so allowing this music to mold me played right into the development of wrong world views and thinking. Again- *"The heart is deceitful above all things, and desperately sick; who can understand it?"*Jeremiah 17:9 ESV

CHAPTER 3
"SEED IS SOWN"

Spiritual Identity- The Spirit

1974 - Spring 1983

German Roots

There was one more element to help shape another one of my identities growing up, and that element was the church. The culture around me through movies and music was influencing me a lot and developing my soul realm, which is how I think and reason, my will and my emotions. But the church came into play and was developing my spirit and started to develop my view of God and the Bible. All three of these identities, my bass identity, my soul identity and my spirit identity would fight for my attention. I found that this identity would be the most important one as I got older.

At the age of 5, I told my parents that I wanted to be a Pastor. And not only a Pastor but I wanted to be a German Pastor. My imagination as a young boy was very alive- that's for sure. I would imagine what it would be like to live in Germany. I remember thinking the German language was the coolest language on the face of the earth. I wanted to learn it because after all I was going to 'preach the Gospel in German'. My parents got me this book on how to speak German. I set in my mind that I was going to go to Germany and be a Pastor.

My family has a lot of German roots on my mom's side. We would frequently go to Frankenmuth, Michigan, which was a tourist town of the German culture. They would have German food, beer, and shops. Even the waitresses had to dress the part in German attire. There is this cool store called Bronners that my mom and dad would love to go to. We would shop there every year and get Christmas ornaments or other decorations, and eat at the famous Zender's, which was a German restaurant with German recipes. I loved the food there.

Christmas Eve Roots

There was a tradition of my parents taking us kids to my Grandma and Grandpa's on Christmas Eve for dinner, which was always delicious. When we would get done eating, we would head over to Messiah Lutheran Church in Clio, Michigan, and attend one of the Christmas Eve services they offered that night. This is the church that my grandparents, along with most of my Mom's side of the family, would go to. It was always a great feeling of going to this Christmas Eve service. When I would walk into the church, I would have an expectation that good things were going to happen. Being it was a Lutheran church, there was that tradition of German roots.

I knew the music was always top-notch, Messiah Lutheran for this service. Even as a young boy I was excited to hear the music they were preparing. The organ and band were always spot on, and the choir was always exceptional. They also had a handbell choir that I just loved. I don't know what it was about the sound of those bells, but they just brought joy to my soul listening to them.

We would always end the service with the song "Silent Night." One of my favorite songs to sing to this day. At the beginning of the service, they would pass out candles. At the end of the service, they would have ushers light the candles of those on the outside of the pew and each person would pass the flame of their lit candle to the next person. We would start to sing that song and it was like my heart would light up with joy. The choir would sing, and the harmonies were fantastic. My Dad would sing his heart out on this song every time.

I realized that my Dad loved to sing, and he would not hold back when he sang these Christmas songs. It was at that point I realized that wow, my Dad could really sing. He would sing these Christmas songs like he owned them. I remember as a kid I thought that was the coolest thing ever. One thing that I picked up on is whenever my Dad was singing there was a passion that he let out to show how much he loved to sing. This is where I started to develop a love for music. I thought this church music was awesome and my Dad was a rock star. I mean hey, I was a young boy.

I loved to sing melodies to the Christmas songs, especially the song "What Child Is This." That is my all-time favorite Christmas song to sing. It was about the melody more than anything. The verses had this waltzy-flow to the rhythm, and when it came to the chorus, it would go up high to the words, *"This, this is Christ the King,Whom shepherds guard and Angel's sing - Haste, haste, to bring Him laud,The Babe, the Son of Mary."* I loved, and still do to this day, singing those words - and I made a connection with this melody.

Another Christmas song that made a huge impact on me was "O Come All Ye Faithful." This song again has one of the best Christmas melodies. I still love singing the whole song of melody. It reminds me of a violin-type melody. The way it jumps around and how rhythmic it is, along with being very dynamic. These two songs, as well as some others, would start to develop my ear to what kind of melodies and chord progressions I would like in music. Especially when I started to write music.

Sunday School

Sunday school was always a great experience for me. I remember as far back as 4 years old being in the church basement and having fun learning stories of the Bible. I always thought it was really cool because the stories of the Bible always ended with God having His way and everything being ok. Abraham and Sarah finally have a child. Noah building a cool ark, putting tons of animals on it with his family, and floating around for a while. Moses and the children of God being set free, then wandering around in the desert before they finally got to the promised land. My favorite one was about David and Goliath. I mean, who doesn't like the story of a young boy getting in a fight with someone 3x his size, yet winning the fight. As a kid I didn't really understand the spiritual aspect of the stories of the Bible, but they were heartwarming and made me feel good.

It was cool learning all these Bible stories, but when I was 9 years old there was a particular lesson I really connected with. That lesson was how to share Jesus with others. My Sunday school teacher laid out 4 weeks of what the gospel was and what the Bible says on how to share it. These were the most exciting classes out of all the time I spent in Sunday school. I was hanging on her every word of teaching, and was taking it all in. At the time, I didn't know why I was so excited about these particular Sunday school classes.

In the last class of the 4-week lesson plan, she summarized what we went over. Repent, Jesus died for you, your sins are forgiven, he was resurrected. For some reason that just made total sense to me in my head. Then after she summarized it, my Sunday school teacher challenged us to find someone to share the gospel with. She then told us that the next week we will share with each other what happened. I was so excited and couldn't wait to do this. I had the person already in mind who I was going to share the gospel with.

First Time Sharing The Gospel

I was ready to share just like my Sunday school teacher wanted me to do. I told my parents what I was doing and who I wanted to share the gospel with. He was a neighborhood friend of mine. I knew that he really didn't go to church so I made up in my mind that he would be a prime candidate to hear the gospel. I called him up to see if he wanted to get together. He agreed to get together and hang out.

I was super nervous about sharing the gospel because I knew he could reject this idea of becoming a Christian and making Jesus Lord. I was going over what to say and how to say it. I walked over to his house. It was a beautiful sunny day; I do remember that. We started walking down the street and I was really anxious about this. I finally mustered up enough courage to start this conversation about Jesus.

I really don't remember everything that I said. I just remember that I tried to follow what my Sunday school teacher said. We had a conversation about what sin was and how Jesus has forgiven our sin. Then I remember asking him if Jesus was his Lord and Savior. He told me that He is not. I asked him if he wanted to know Jesus and come to church with me.

Now you might think that this story would end with my friend coming to church with me and we have those warm fuzzies of a good ending. After I asked him if he wanted to know Jesus and come to church, he started laughing hysterically. Then he went on to say that he didn't need Jesus and church was useless. I didn't know what to say. I wasn't trained for this. I was just a 9-year-old kid wanting to share the gospel with someone. I did not expect the intense push back. I felt as though I failed and was embarrassed by the whole situation. I went home rejected.

I was just so upset because I really thought it

would be so easy. Just like I was taught to present the gospel to the person - then the person will say yes. It's that simple right? Obviously not! I didn't even think that someone might say no to the gospel. I remember he said that his family didn't believe in Jesus, and they were atheists. This was a strange thing to hear and take in. Everyone I knew seemed like they were Christian or at least was ok with Christianity. To hear someone reject the Gospel was something I didn't know how to handle.

The following week I wasn't looking forward to going to Sunday school class because I was embarrassed that I failed. I didn't want to hear everyone else's success story and then mine. I felt like a loser. The class time started, and I came to find out I was the only one who tried to share. She didn't ask what happened she just told me good job and encouraged us all to be intentional in sharing the gospel when we are ready to do so. I was relieved.

Faith Challenged

I was about 11 years old, and I asked my Sunday school teacher this question: Who made God? Who is God's father? Initially the Sunday school teacher was telling me that we just need to believe that God existed. In my mind that was not good enough. Logically God had to have parents and I wanted to know who created Him. The Sunday school teacher did the right thing and said that we could talk about this more after class the next week. I thought to myself how wonderful it will be to know who God's parents are the following week.

I couldn't grab the concept that God just existed and created everything like the story in Genesis. This idea of Creation perplexed me, how is it that God spoke everything into existence. "Let there be light and there was light", how is that so. How is it that man was created out of the dust and God breathed life into him. A lifeless body God gave life. How is this so? This made no sense to me at all.

The following week I tried to look around when I was outdoors and imagine how this tree was spoken into existence or the birds of the air. Birds fascinated me. Growing up I lived next to a field that had a lot of pheasants. Such a beautiful bird and I would always admire the colors and they displayed as they would make themselves known flying out of the field. Then there were the stars. Many nights I would look up at the sky at night and wonder how it all came into existence.

The next week came, and I was excited to talk more about this concept rolling around in my head of "who are God's parents? Where did He come from?" I remember my Sunday school teacher sitting me down and sharing with me what it means to put my faith in God. That I had to have faith that God existed and that we cannot fully understand everything, but we can put our faith in Him and believe that what the Bible says is true. I'll admit, it wasn't what I was hoping for, but I took her guidance to just know that I had to try and simply have faith and believe.

Over the next several weeks I started to just think about what it meant to have faith. And that led to more questions. I would have robust conversations with my Sunday school teacher about faith. She told me a modern-day parable.

She asked, "Do you have faith that if I sat in a chair, it would hold me."

I said, "Yes I do."

She then said, "You wouldn't think about whether it would hold you?"

I said, "I might take a quick look at it and make sure nothing is cracked or something."

She then asked "What about a chair you know is ok? Would you just sit in it without questioning whether it is, ok?"

I said "Well, yes I would".

Then she went on to point out how I have faith in a chair to hold me not knowing where it was made, who assembled it or exactly what materials they used.

She then said, "It is the same as having faith in God, we don't know who made Him, or where He came from, or what He is made of, but we know He exists, and we put our faith in Him".

I remember after this conversation with my

Sunday school teacher that I wanted to agree with her but there was another something inside of me that was casting doubt. Something inside me told me that my Sunday school teacher was wrong, and I should keep questioning God's existence. This is my first recollection of a conflict within me between the authority of the church and my conscience/soul. I remember walking out of the church that day with this strange confidence-like a sense of arrogance.

Confirmation Class

Soon after that I started attending confirmation classes. This would be four years of learning Martin Luther's Catechism and developing my spiritual identity with foundational doctrine as a Lutheran. Even though I questioned God's existence, I was really excited to get into these classes. This was a big deal to me.

When I found out the Pastor was going to challenge us to memorize Bible verses every week, I became ecstatic. My church, Holy Cross, buys the class Bibles to study out of for confirmation classes. This particular Bible was called *The Way*, and it was the New Living Translation version, which made it easy to understand. I actually still have that Bible. Over the next four years of confirmation classes, we would spend a lot of time memorizing Bible verses and Creeds. This would spark a desire in me to know the Bible the best I could. I started to have a strong desire to know the Word of God.

Every spring, Holy Cross would have a service dedicated to recognizing the confirmands. It was like a graduation. During this service everyone who was being confirmed would have to recite creeds from the Martin Luther's Catechism. I remember being so nervous before the service because I didn't want to mess up the creed I had to recite. I was so relieved when I recited the creed and didn't make a mistake. I really didn't understand what the creed meant but it didn't matter it - was cool reciting something hundreds of years old.

Everyone who was confirmed received a confirmation verse as well. The verse I received was Psalm 37:4 *"Take delight in the Lord, and he will give you your heart's desire. Commit everything you do to the Lord, trust Him, and he will help you."* During the service the Pastor would have you kneel at the altar lay his hands on your head and speak your confirmation verse over you. I thought that was one of the coolest things to ever happen to me. The idea of a spiritual leader affirming that I did something right and speaking words from an ancient book, that for some reason I had a desire to learn, was amazing for me at 13 years old.

My parents had a confirmation party for me after the service. I was nervously excited because I was hoping to get enough money to go and buy a bass amp. So many people showed up to my confirmation party. I remember shaking a lot of hands and talking to a lot of people I didn't really know. As I opened the cards given to me, I became excited because I received enough money to get this bass amp I wanted. The most important gift I received was from my Mom and Dad though. It was a silver chain with a silver cross and a medallion that had a cross on one side and the saying "I am Lutheran" on the other side. It was a memorable day.

Something Happened

I had 3 identities I identified with up to this point in my life. I had my identity as a bass player (body), my identity as a rocker (soul), and now my identity as a church goer (spirit). I was accelerating on bass and the music I listened to was influencing my worldview and forming my thinking. Now this identity as a church goer was also in the mix. I had knowledge about the Bible, but I really did not 'know' the Bible. I could talk a good game and recite some things, but I had no understanding of what I was taught.

After confirmation I still had a desire to learn more about God and the Bible. The ability to continue learning about God and the Bible at my church through group study came to a halt after I was confirmed. I remember my Dad taking me up to the church and talking to the Pastor about a high school Bible study. For whatever reason my church did not offer a high school youth program to keep it going after confirmation. I was really bummed out because I was really hoping for a continued Bible study after the confirmation classes.

The next best thing to do was to pay attention to the Pastor on Sunday morning. I would listen to the Pastor, but I really didn't understand what he was saying. I would pay more attention to the Scripture readings than the sermon. Lutherans read three Scriptures every Sunday morning. One from the Old Testament, one from the Epistles, and then one from the Gospels. I always listened closely to try and get what was being said. I would always try and get a bulletin so I could follow along on the Scripture readings. I especially liked it when the readings dealt with the idea of good and evil, demons and angels. I would try and keep the bulletins and take them home if they had a Scripture that caught my attention.

So as time went on, I found myself thinking too much about things that went against the authorities in my life and not thinking about God and the Bible as much. Then something I was unfamiliar with introduced themself to me. It was like a voice of reason. I really never thought about doing things that went against the authority of my parents or the church, but here I was in this dilemma. The voice of reason started to tell me that it was not a bad thing to want to start drinking beer or start smoking cigarettes. After all, I deserve it right? I should be able to do what I want. If it feels good, do it, right? It started to convince me that it was ok to think this way. Seems to make sense to me.

I started to dwell on these things and my desires started to change. It was like something was waiting for me to be done with confirmation classes knowing that after I was done, they could persuade me to think differently. I mean it was logical that I rebel against authority because I identified as a rocker. I started to desire to drink and smoke. Heck, I even wanted to have a girlfriend. I guess that is normal for any middle school boy going into high school.

With this going on it felt like there was a fight of good and evil pushing each other around inside of myself. I could feel this struggle all the time. Almost like there was a battle for attention. Who would I pay attention to? The desire to rebel against the authority, or the desire to draw close to God. Back and forth, back and forth, which one would get my attention. It really depended on the day. Let's be honest, the less time you spend with something or someone the less desirable it/they become. It's just how we are wired as a humans. **What we spend our time thinking about is what we will end up doing and becoming like.**

It really shouldn't be too surprising though because growing up I had all this music that had the concept of hell or devil in the lyrics influencing me right alongside the time spent learning about God through my church. The two identities grew up together with me. They both have influenced me and were wanting my attention. **Whichever desire is nurtured is the one we, meaning human beings, will follow.**

The Word Was Sown

"The sower sows the word." Mark 4:14

Growing up in the church, while attending Sunday school and also going through confirmation classes, was a time of God sowing seed into my life as a young boy. The Pastors at Holy Cross Lutheran Church and Messiah Lutheran Church sowed the seed of God's word into my life through their sermons. I really didn't understand what the Pastors were trying to say when they gave their sermons, but nonetheless, the seed was being sown even though the lesson of the sermon went way over my head.

The bulletins were also a source of sowing the word of God into my life because there were Scripture readings in them. I can't really explain it, but for some reason those bulletins were something I really liked to take home with me. I would always ask my Dad if he could get an extra one. I would read the bulletin and try to figure out what it was saying. I really liked the idea of learning what the Scriptures were saying, especially when they talked about angels and demons.

But the biggest season of the seed sowing of God's word was the confirmation classes I went to in middle school. In these classes we took the time to actually study the Bible and memorize Scriptures, Creeds and the service liturgy. I started to feel like I was connecting with something as if I could find my identity of value, purpose and worth.

So as God's Word was being sown did it take root? Did the Word of God penetrate the soil of my heart? That's a tough question to answer. I'm going to say in my case, maybe some seed did sorta, but it did not take root, meaning it did not establish itself in my heart (spirit). We know that seed must take root for it to grow, right? Some seed of God's Word was snatched up right away and some may have started to take root, but before it could establish itself, it died. Look at this parable Jesus shared in Luke to better understand what I am saying:

"And when a great crowd was gathering and people from town after town came to him, he said in a parable, "A sower went out to sow his seed. And as he sowed, some fell along the path and was trampled underfoot, and the birds of the air devoured it. And

some fell on the rock, and as it grew up, it withered away, because it had no moisture. And some fell among thorns, and the thorns grew up with it and choked it. And some fell into good soil and grew and yielded a hundredfold." As he said these things, he called out, "He who has ears to hear, let him hear." Luke 8:4-8 ESV

"Now the parable is this: The seed is the word of God. The ones along the path are those who have heard; then the devil comes and takes away the word from their hearts, so that they may not believe and be saved. And the ones on the rock are those who, when they hear the word, receive it with joy. But these have no root; they believe for a while, and in time of testing fall away. And as for what fell among the thorns, they are those who hear, but as they go on their way they are choked by the cares and riches and pleasures of life, and their fruit does not mature. As for that in the good soil, they are those who, hearing the word, hold it fast in an honest and good heart, and bear fruit with patience." Luke 8:11-15 ESV

Heart Was Hard

My heart was like the hard ground and the shallow soil. Most of the lessons I learned were snatched up by the devil and it had no chance to take root. The areas of my heart where there was some usable soil would not be deep enough for the root of the Word to become established.

I would receive the seed of the Word with joy through Bible study. This would be exciting, and I wanted to learn more and keep it going after I was confirmed. But the challenges to grow the seed became very hard due to the lack of knowledge and leadership. This would cause any root of the planted seed to dry up and die.

The biggest challenge was the next fall when Bible studies started up at church again. I realized that there were no plans for high schoolers to have a Bible study and connect with any type of church leader. I'm not sure if that was a Lutheran thing or if my church just didn't have the resources to have a Bible study for high schoolers. I remember talking to my Dad about this and he became concerned as well, so we both headed up to the church one evening to talk to the Pastor. He was surprised there was nothing for high schoolers to continue with Bible study. Then what happened was any seed that took root inside me couldn't establish itself and start to grow. Instead, it withered and died. My excitement and joy were deflated which in turn killed any desire.

There were certain things that I would not forget even though my desire for God was deflated. Some of what I learned I was able to commit to memory. Like the Apostles Creed, the Lord's Prayer, as well as some of the service Liturgy. This would prove to be instrumental down the road for the Holy Spirit to use for my reconciliation to God the Father.

As the sower sows the seed, there is no way of telling whether the seed is being devoured, withering, being choked or taking root. The obedience of those Sunday school teachers and Bible study teachers would prove to bring a harvest later down the road. They trusted that the Holy Spirit would water it and somewhere down the line the seed would take root and be established.

As the Body of Christ, we do not know how the seed takes root and grows to full maturity, but it's not our job to figure that out. Our job as the Body of Christ is to be obedient to sow the seed and not worry about which soil the seed is going into. Simply throw the seed out there through Bible teaching, Bible study, encouragement, and listening. That is what the Sunday school teachers did along with confirmation classes at Holy Cross Lutheran Church. They sowed seeds. I'm very thankful for their obedience to share God's Word and teach it not only to me, but to all the kids that they taught throughout the years.

Here is a parable to sum this up. *"And he said, "The kingdom of God is as if a man should scatter seed on the ground. He sleeps and rises night and day, and the seed sprouts and grows; he knows not how. The earth produces by itself, first the blade, then the ear, then the full grain in the ear. But when the grain is ripe, at once he puts in the sickle, because the harvest has come.""*Mark 4:26-29 ESV

But, because there was no direction for

me, my desire for God faded fast. This became an opportunity for the devil to pounce and water the seed he already sowed in me through the music I was connecting with at that time in my life. The devil would sow more seed into me that go against God's Word. If you do not think the devil is looking for an opportunity, you are kidding yourself. I was an easy target. Isn't that what lions do when they hunt is find the easy target and pounce. The devil knew I would not be able to push back because the Word of God did not have sufficient root for me to know who I am In Christ. 1 Peter 5:8 ESV *"Be sober-minded; be watchful. Your adversary the devil prowls around like a roaring lion, seeking someone to devour."*

The battlefield was my heart. Right around the time I started confirmation classes was about the time I started to listen to all that music with hell or the devil in the lyrics. Coincidence? I don't think so. It was all in time and in step together. It would be a constant battle for my heart, which in the Greek -*Kardia* translates to 'inner man' or 'your mind.' Even though seeds of the Word of God was being snatched up and not taking root, some seed would make it to good soil. God made sure of that. And God would use that seed later on, down the road of my life.

The devil cannot go up against the Word of God when it has taken root and grown to the point of understanding. That is why he works hard at devouring the seed before it has a chance of taking root. If the seed takes root, then that will lead to gaining understanding of God's Word which then leads to salvation. The Bible says the Word saves you. *"So get rid of all the filth and evil in your lives, and humbly accept the word God has planted in your hearts, for it has the power to save your souls."*James 1:21 NLT

When the devil attacks Jesus, we see that He simply uses the Word of God to put the devil in his place. I say again the devil cannot stand against the Word of God. *"Then the devil said to him, "If you are the Son of God, tell this stone to become a loaf of bread." But Jesus told him, "No! The Scriptures say, 'People do not live by bread alone.'" Then the devil took him up and revealed to him all the kingdoms of the world in a moment of time. "I will give you the glory of these kingdoms and authority over them," the devil said, "because they are mine to give to anyone I please. I will give it all to you if you will worship me." Jesus replied, "The Scriptures say, 'You must worship the Lord your God and serve only him.'" Then the devil took him to Jerusalem, to the highest point of the Temple, and said, "If you are the Son of God, jump off! For the Scriptures say, 'He will order his angels to protect and guard you. And they will hold you up with their hands so you won't even hurt your foot on a stone.'" Jesus responded, "The Scriptures also say, 'You must not test the Lord your God.'" When the devil had finished tempting Jesus, he left him until the next opportunity came."*Luke 4:3-13 NLT

CHAPTER 4
"BATTLE BEGINS"

Spiritual Identity - The Occult

Summer 1983- Summer 1985

Witchcraft

In light of the pondering of the battle of good and evil I started to seriously think about whether male witches really existed, because if they did, I wanted to become one and try spell casting. Remember I didn't have Google back in 1983, just saying. I wondered where this desire for witchcraft was coming from. As I would hang out with these new friends, I made in my freshman year of high school, the topic of witchcraft would come up often. I became very interested in what they were saying. I asked them if males could be witches, they said Yes!! This stirred up the desire of becoming a warlock to the forefront of my thinking. I just thought this was the coolest thing ever at the age of 14. They saw I was interested so they invited me to join their 'witches coven' and some even had parents that were witches. My first reaction was how cool would that be.

I started to think about this all the time starting what a warlock's attire would be. The pictures I saw of warlocks at that time they were wearing long black leather trench coats and had long hair and sunglasses. Anyway, I started to think about how to get a long black leather trench coat. After all, isn't that what warlocks wear, according to the media and movies? They also wear cool sunglasses!! I had to look the part, I guess. I was bummed out though when I realized that I wouldn't be able to join that witch coven because I couldn't drive a car. I never got the leather trench coat, but I did score some cool sunglasses. I didn't think that my parents would buy me a trench coat or want to take me to a witch coven to practice witchcraft.

Even though I could not go to the witches' coven, one of those friends in the group took it upon herself to introduce me to spell casting. I thought to myself, now I'm getting somewhere. She told me that she got her spells from spell books. I asked her how she knew of these books, and she went on to tell me that her mom was a witch and she had spell casting books that she used. Then she told me that she engages in casting spells all the time over people and situations. I was like, what are you talking about? How does this work?

She explained how she would recognize something she wanted to change in her life to have a desirable outcome. Then she would go and find a spell to match her desire by using her mom's spell casting books. After she found the spell, she would then cast the spell.

I asked her if I could cast spells and she said I could. I flipped out. Finally, I am going to find out what this spell casting is all about. She took it upon herself to offer to bring some spells from her mom's spell books for me to try out. I thought that was very cool. She asked me what are some things that I want to see changed, like relationships, or grades or really anything. I thought about it and then told her I wanted to have a girlfriend and have people like me.

The next day she brings in these spells and gives them to me to try. I asked her if there was anything I should do or should I say it a certain way or what? She just told me to say the spell like I believed it and that was it. I thought to myself that I can do that. I took the spells home and read over them to make sure I didn't stumble over the words. Then I spoke them out of my mouth like I knew what I was doing. I didn't feel any different or have any spiritual experience. I just said the spell and that was it.

A few days later she would ask me how

things were going and if I saw any of my spell casting come to pass the way I wanted. I really didn't see any change as the days went on. I told her not yet. She tried telling me that it could take a while before I would see things happen. I was bummed out because I really didn't see the results that I wanted. I expected this big magical experience and just like on TV I would be able to manipulate my situation to be in my favor.

You could say I struck out with joining a witch's coven and doing the spell casting. I did not get anything out of it that I was hoping for. And somehow, I got this friend in trouble from her mom for sharing those spells with me so that avenue to learn witchcraft became a dead end. Even though I struck out learning witchcraft at that time in my life, the desire would still be there. I thought maybe some day I could learn this practice of spell casting.

The Music (Fall 1983)

Around the same timeframe at the age of 14 I started to really get into a heavier sound with the music I listened too. I was introduced to heavy metal. Bands like Judas Priest, Quiet Riot, Motley Crew, Ozzy Osbourne, Scorpions, Accept and a lot of other bands. I've been listening to rock bands up to this point and started to venture into the sound of the heavy metal and screaming vocals. I didn't replace the rock genre I was listening to; this new heavy metal genre was an addition to the rock genre I already loved to listen to since I made that decision at 10 years old to be a rocker.

This new heavy metal sound that I discovered became my new favorite type of music. In November 1983 Ozzy Osbourne's song "Bark at the Moon" came out and it instantly became my favorite jam. Something about that album and that song specifically started to make me think different. It was a continuation of how the song "See You In Hell" made me feel. Like I was becoming more comfortable with the dark side.

I remember when I bought the album, the picture of Ozzy on the cover was chilling to me. He looked like Linda Blair from the movie *The Exorcist*. He looked possessed! I always like Ozzy's solo albums and he looked possessed on the other two album covers but *Bark at the Moon* triggered something in me. It caused me to think deeper about good and evil, demons and angels. Every time I would listen to that song "Bark at the Moon," I would stare at that album cover in a daze like I was making a connection to something not of myself.

I remember that year when this song came out (1983) we were all getting ready for Christmas Eve to go to my grandparents. I was having one of those moments where I was so into this song, I was jamming it in my room over and over. My parents were like "Let's go, what's taking you so long?" Of course, being a 'I know everything teenager' I was wanting to do my own thing. I was actually upset with them for being upset with me.

But I remember the car ride out to my grandparents that night. I stared out the window pondering the idea of the spirit realm around me. I was questioning the idea of whether demons existed or not, but deep inside me I already knew they did. I wondered if all this desire to connect with the dark side was a real desire. Why was I desiring to be a part of all this darkness. Even though trying the spell casting didn't seem to work out I still wanted to be a warlock spell caster.

I ended up thinking a lot about good vs evil that night especially at the Christmas Eve service we went to after dinner. We always went to Clio Messiah Lutheran Church for Christmas Eve service. It was a tradition in our family. Hearing the Christmas story is something that was presented clearly at this service every year. I thought about how the angel Gabriel spoke to Joseph and Mary about the birth of Jesus and how the angels protected them from danger after He was born. I thought why the dark side couldn't overcome the good. My mind was really reeling that night.

I started to look at what this song "Bark at the Moon" actually had to say in the lyrics. When I looked at the lyrics to this song, to me, it came across as an evil presence breaking free from the 'mouth of hell.' Like it was forcefully put there by a bully or oppressor. In my 14-year-old mind being strong armed by the devil, I thought is it possible that God was the bully?

That led me to think that maybe God is the enemy then. Maybe that's why the devil was trying to ruin Christmas because God would always bully him. What was deemed as good must actually be evil then. Needless to say, I was very confused and in my own mind I was starting to see evil as good and good as evil. Where was all this coming from? It definitely was not of myself.

Shout At The Devil (Spring 1984)

While that thought process was developing in my mind there were new songs that I would start to connect with. One of them was "Shout At The Devil" by Motley Crew. One of the things that I initially liked about this song was the music. The bass tone was awesome, and I wanted to emulate my bass tone after Motley Crews bass player. Vince Neil's vocals were very cool and would demand my attention as well. Every time that song was played on the radio, I cranked it up. Of course, it was a song with the word hell or devil in the title. Like a non-questioning sheep, I was drawn to that song. It was similar to the *Bark at the Moon* album and really had the same theme: devil, hell, anti-God. What a surprise!

I read articles in magazines that the

backstory of the song was Nikki Sixx was practicing Satanism when he wrote this song. There are interviews online of those close to Nikki Sixx that claim they saw some real strange things, like flying silverware while eating dinner. Some believed that he was tapping into something very dark. For some reason those kinds of stories attracted me more to that type of music. I loved the lyrics of this song, and of course the chorus of the song I would scream at the top of my lungs, like all the other songs. I mean in my mind I thought it was such a great chorus to actually shout. Just like the chorus was telling me to do. So, I did! I shouted at the devil.

And then just like every other song, I paid attention to the verses after I learned the chorus of the song. Which in the music business they call "the hook." I went back and read the verses of the song. As I listened to the verses of "Shout at the Devil," I interpreted them to talk about desire. How the devil would be that desire or make things better if he is involved with what you are doing. I was learning to do whatever made me feel good and was developing a desire to serve myself. I am number one, stay 'true' to myself, 'I' need to be happy and satisfied. This was yet another song influencing my way of thinking.

Attitude Changed

That summer after school got out things started to really change inside of me. Of course, music was influencing me, and you could say it was being my guide. Yet, another band would again make me think. Dio came out with an album called *Holy Diver*. This album is where I started to develop a rebellious attitude against organized churches. The album cover alone was setting off this attitude. The cover is a demon swinging a chain over its head and this chain is attached to a priest being cast into a sea of water.

The title track "Holy Diver" was musically stellar but the lyrics, as Dio himself explains, talks about his negative upbringing in the Catholic church. He explained that he experienced oppression and manipulation from the Catholic Church as a child to just simply believe what they taught. He did not agree with the tactics of the Catholic Church. Knowing this, something just rose up inside me where I was angry. In my mind I started to see the church as being a bully. I already was seeing God as a bully and now the church.

The anger came from me hating being bullied myself. I felt like this song was stirring up something inside me to want and protect myself from being bullied from the church, or as we called them back then, "religious freaks." I would express my emotion towards the "religious freaks" by cursing them out and exposing their logic as being in error. I saw the church a repressor of desires. I mean why would anyone want to repress my desires. Who would do that?

It was in the news and written articles that the “religious freaks" were attacking the music that I listened to. It started in 1982, and there was a claim that if you played certain songs backwards there was a message from Satan. Beatle songs, Led Zeppelin's “Stairway to Heaven,” and others. The evangelical church was actually trying to prove this claim for a few years before I even heard about it. This would set off a rebellious anger within me. I felt like I was at war with these repressors. I started to see the church as a bad option.

My parents were disciplined to go to church every Sunday, so I would go because my parents would go, (thanks for doing that Mom and Dad, for real). I still enjoyed the traditions and liturgy of the services because I liked the music, but I would zone out on the sermon. I just put-up walls to protect against any attacks that might come my way. This is how I felt. It was like a love hate relationship with the church. On one hand God and His church were repressing my freedoms, on the other hand I liked the traditions and music of the church. I was confused for sure.

My church Holy Cross Lutheran Church did not specifically attack me, but I didn’t want to take a chance. I felt as though I had to protect the ideology of what was developing in me and justify the music I listened to. After all, this music that I listened to was my life. I felt like the music was a part of me and I had to take a stand against the opposition and be ready. Strangely enough I felt like I was at war with the church, and I was preparing myself to take on any attacks. This newly found ideology and attitude from the devil planting seeds would start to take root in my life.

Wrote Paper - Fall 1984

There was this English class that I took that year, and it was a class where I had the opportunity to learn how to write essays or short research papers. The first paper I wrote was about the bass players I looked up to at that time, John Paul Jones, Chris Squire and Steve Harris. The teacher wanted me to write about something else, but he finally agreed that it would be ok to write about these bass players' lives. We had a robust disagreement as to whether the word 'bassist' was an actual word or not. I said it was and he argued it was not. I used magazines like *Hit Parader* to back my claim. He said those magazines were not a reliable source. I don't know, maybe he was right.

The second paper I wrote for that class was really making waves. I decided I wanted to write about the oppression religious freaks tried to put on teenagers like me. I was very passionate about how I felt on this topic. I would vent to a classmate, Pam, in my Spanish class about how I hated the religious freaks. I don't think she knew what to say, probably because she wasn't interested in this topic. Nonetheless, she sat and listened to me ramble on about this topic. It was like I had to tell anyone who would listen to me about how religious freaks are bad people and she was nice enough to to listen to me.

I hand my paper in with the expectation the teacher would give me a good grade. He gave me a C which I thought was a punishment. I guess he said I was too opinionated and couldn't back my claim. He was right, but I was still upset. Pam had to hear how my teacher was punishing me for my opinion and how those religious freaks are terrible people for forcing their views on us teenagers. Poor girl, she was a trooper though and just let me talk.

This attitude of being anti-church and hating repressors would mold my attitude for my high school experience. I wasn't a satanist, or evil person, I just started to have an opinion of things. I hated oppression and really thought the religious freaks were doing this. This would set the tone for things to come. Seeing evil as good and good as evil already had taken root but, the root was going deeper in me.

Praying To Satan - Spring 1985

I was seeing evil as good, and voices would come to my head. I was hearing voices for a while so this wasn't anything new to me, but these voices were more conversational and opinionated. One thing that they focused on with me was to gain my trust. Trying to get me to simply have a conversation with them like they were real. Well- they were real.

Now if you never had voices come into your head it can be kinda scary. This would be the first time I would take these voices seriously. Now maybe some of you are joking about hearing voices. Maybe you're saying something like "The voices are calling" in a joking manner. People let me tell you something, if someone says to you that they have voices in their head do not make fun of them. Voices are a real thing for many people in this world, including me.

After a while these voices became a part of my daily routine. They kept talking to me like I was a friend or something. At this time in my life, it was important to have friends. You could say I was becoming friends with these voices. They would talk to me in the morning before school and talk to me throughout the day. Sometimes they would even say goodnight to me. During these times I started to reason with them and actually thought that what these voices were saying to me made sense at times. I have to admit I liked the idea of voices talking to me. It seemed to bring some sort of comfort. I was looking at them as a friend.

One day one of the voices started telling me

he could give me what my heart wants. Of course, I was intrigued so I asked "how?" He wouldn't tell me right away he just kept telling me that he could give me what I want. I kept asking how and he kept avoiding answering me. Then the voice finally decided I should know how I could get what I want. It was like he was leading up to the answer by teasing me. It was one of those moments that went like this, "you want to know,' "yes", "you sure you want to know" and I would be like "just tell me already."

Then the voice said, "Ok this is what you have to do...ready.... just ask Satan to give you what you want, and he will." When I first heard that I was kinda freaked out. I mean this voice was telling me to pray to the devil. At first, I was like "no I am not going to do that." But the voice stayed persistent and started to reason with me how it was OK to pray to Satan and would not let up. Something did not feel right about doing this, so I had to think about what was going on here.

Then one day as I was reasoning in my mind about praying to the devil and I started to have this conversation: I started to think about whether or not I would be damned to hell if I prayed to Satan. All of a sudden, a voice popped up and said "why worry about that? Is it because of hell? It is no big deal, remember? It is not the fire and brimstone you were taught by your church." Then I thought "what about God?' Then the voice said, "Yes what about God, He has done nothing for you." Believe it or not this voice was making sense to me.

I still couldn't shake that something was telling me it was not a good idea to pray to the devil. Then all of a sudden something inside me caused me to feel that I needed to resist this line of thinking and that praying to the devil was a good idea. I made up my mind that I was going to pray to the devil. I found myself initiating conversations with these voices like I was looking for them because I wanted to know how to pray to Satan. A voice finally chimed in, and I asked the voice how to do this. He explained to me how to do it. It was not rocket science; he just told me to ask for what I wanted. Whatever my desire was. When I got past being nervous and I made a list of my desires. I prayed for the biggest fleshly desires on my heart. I wanted to be popular and have a girlfriend. I remember when I was done praying for that I felt different. It was like I had this overwhelming sense of confidence like I was unstoppable. Arrogance comes to mind.

Seed Devoured

"The ones along the path are those who have heard; then the devil comes and takes away the word from their hearts, so that they may not believe and be saved." Luke 8:12

This was a crazy two years of my life. Where was God through all this? Why did it seem that God gave up on me at such an early age and let me have all these occult desires? After all, isn't He sovereign? Couldn't he have removed me from all the situations that came up and the temptations that were presented? I mean, I guess so. But as I look back, I am so thankful that I would have these experiences. What are you talking about Mike? Let me explain.

Like any 13-year-old boy, I was very impressionable and an open book to allow influence, whether good or bad, to mold me. I was an easy target for the devil, like a sheep on the mountainside with no one to protect me. I was vulnerable and didn't know any better and I was ignorant of the Word of God. It was the devil's turn to try and take the seed he planted over the years and establish it in my heart.

The biggest thing the devil did was take out the competition of Bible teaching by deflating my desire and "taking the seed away." The seed didn't even have a chance to take root. Because of this I was not able to understand the things of God and what to believe- it kept me ignorant to God's Word. This opened the door for my mind to be influenced by the devil as he would try and get me to submit to occultism type ideas.

He Will Deceive You

The devil had to try and create that interest within me by deceiving me. Up to this point in my life I was more intrigued by the idea of the occult and not a participator. As he first removed the desire for God by devouring any seed sown in me, he would now have to convince me that the occult was a good idea. He reasoned with me that God was a fraud and that he, the devil, was out for my best interests.

We find in Genesis 3 the tactic the devil has used to deceive God's people since Adam and Eve were created *"Now the serpent was more crafty than any other beast of the field that the Lord God had made. He said to the woman, "Did God actually say, 'You shall not eat of any tree in the garden'?" And the woman said to the serpent, "We may eat of the fruit of the trees in the garden, but God said, 'You shall not eat of the fruit of the tree that is in the midst of the garden, neither shall you touch it, lest you die.'" But the serpent said to the woman, "You will not surely die. For God knows that when you eat of it your eyes will be opened, and you will be like God, knowing good and evil." So when the woman saw that the tree was good for food, and that it was a delight to the eyes, and that the tree was to be desired to make one wise, she took off its fruit and ate, and she also gave some to her husband who was with her, and he ate."*

Genesis 3:1-6 ESV

Notice what the serpent says to Eve. He starts to create doubt by saying *'Did God really say that?'* and then he twists around what God told Adam and Eve the consequence would be for eating of that tree 'in the midst of the Garden'. God said they would surely die. The serpent reasoned with them and convinced them that the consequence of surely dying would not happen and there was nothing to worry about.

Then notice what happened to Eve: *"So when the woman saw that the tree was good for food, and that it was a delight to the eyes, and that the tree was to be desired to make one wise, she took off its fruit and ate."* Desire was created within her before she disobeyed God's command and ate of the fruit. Desire is always created before one sin through the tactic of deception. Remember this: **You will not do anything for or against God unless desire is first conceived**.

Because I was an easy target the devil was able to easily deceive me to forget about what I learned in confirmation classes, Sunday school and Sunday morning services. Remember just because you're brought up that way doesn't mean that you won't be deceived into thinking like the devil. I obtained knowledge and not understanding. So because of this the devil had a green light to introduce me to all kinds of philosophies and ideologies that go against God's Word.

Influences

Like I mentioned in chapter 2, music has a powerful influence over the mind whether it is a good or bad influence. The music I listened to always had something to do with hell, the devil or spiritual oppression. The songs "Bark at the Moon" and "Shout at the Devil" stirred me up and changed my attitude towards God. I became more of an anti-God kind of person. Not an atheist, not a Satan worshipper but one who would not recommend going to church and getting to know God. I felt as though God was an authority that was trying to control me and tell me how I should think. I didn't like that and saw it as He was oppressing me.

The music I listened to was under attack from the Church at that time in my life. The Church was standing up and speaking out against all the anti-God lyrics and claiming the songs had backwards messages from Satan. Although now I can see clearly that that music did in fact have anti-God lyrics and encouraged the listener to fulfill the desires of the flesh. He wants everyone to have the desire which leads to the behavior of the flesh. We find that we are called not to live in the desires or behavior of the flesh but rather to walk in the Spirit. *"But I say, walk by the Spirit, and you will not gratify the desires of the flesh. For the desires of the flesh are against the Spirit, and the desires of the Spirit are against the flesh, for these are opposed to each other, to keep you from doing the things you want to do. But if you are led by the Spirit, you are not under the law. Now the works of the flesh are evident: sexual immorality, impurity, sensuality, idolatry, sorcery, enmity, strife, jealousy, fits of anger, rivalries, dissensions, divisions, envy, drunkenness, orgies, and things like these. I warn you, as I warned you before, that those who do such things will not inherit the kingdom of God."* Galatians 5:16-21 ESV

The devil's job is to separate you from knowing the Almighty King, the Lord of Hosts, God the Father. The devil cannot make you do anything. He can only tempt and deceive to take the bait of the temptation. He doesn't force you into doing anything. His tactic is to create the desire within you knowing that your flesh will do it and eventually create the habit of sin in your life.

This is why he starts out as young as possible trying to influence you and deceiving you to believe the lies he creates for you. This is what he was doing with me, creating lies for me to believe. I believed those lies hook line and sinker. I was duped into believing that fulfilling the flesh was the right thing to do. I didn't know any better because I only had knowledge of God's Word and not understanding.

Therefore, my desires were becoming the desires for the world and not for God. I was learning to fulfill the desires of the flesh. Which would lead to the behavior of the flesh. God was not in my heart so I would easily submit to the thinking of the world and sin when the opportunity presented itself. I will not sin unless first the desire is created. As the Scriptures say: *"But each person is tempted when he is lured and enticed by his own desire. Then desire when it has conceived gives birth to sin, and sin when it is fully grown brings forth death."* James 1:15

The devil hasn't changed a thing on how to deceive God's creation. He simply reasons with you and gets you to see that 'you deserve this' or 'God is repressing your freedoms'. Listen closely - when you say 'I deserve it' or 'my freedoms are being repressed' you are agreeing with expressive individualism, which is a form of human secularism.

Voices?

Some people might question whether the voices were real, or my imagination. It's not uncommon for people to hear voices. They could come from your own mind or from spirits in the unseen world. I will tell you this, the spirit realm is a real thing and angels and demons are around us daily. The voices I heard were just like talking to another person. I didn't see anything, but there was an obvious voice of reason whether good or bad that existed. The voices I heard were bad and not of God, so therefore they had to be of Satan's kingdom. God would never tell me to pray to His adversary.

It was a time in my life where I was open to anything for the most part. When I started hearing voices of course it freaked me out. I would spend days wondering whether or not I was crazy. I would consult my psychology teacher in high school on the idea of voices in my head. She thought it was interesting but had no advice as to what to do about it. Eventually, I started to become more at ease with these voices. Like we were all becoming friends or something. For some reason, I can't explain why, the voices felt natural like they belonged in my life.

Just like how the serpent reasoned with Eve and deceived her by twisting God's word, these voices did the same with me. The tactic was the same. The voices reasoned with me that praying to Satan was a good idea. I knew it wasn't right but for some reason I still did. **Those voices got me to doubt what I knew was right and convinced me to do something I knew was wrong.**

The Scriptures do talk a lot about our thought life. We are encouraged to renew our mind with the Word of God. I believe this experience of voices deceiving me to pray to Satan is an example as to why we need to renew our mind with the Word of God. I wasn't saved at that point in my life, so I didn't know any better. I had nothing to challenge the reasoning of the voices. Our mind is what Satan attacks and I thank God for His mercy that I only prayed to Satan for a month or two.

I want to remind you of this passage of Scripture to ponder and meditate: "*The weapons we fight with are not the weapons of the world. On the contrary, they have divine power to demolish strongholds. We demolish arguments and every pretension that sets itself up against the knowledge of God, and we take captive every thought to make it obedient to Christ.*" 2 Corinthians 10:4-5 NIV

CHAPTER 5
"HE TRIED TO CLAIM ME"

Spiritual Identity - The Soul -

Summer 1985-1987

Summer Of 1985

School let out for the summer, I go home and crank up Alice Cooper's song "Schools Out," then sit and stare at the walls wondering what I am going to do that summer. Well, I guess a whole lot would happen. As I got to know some people, one person I was getting to know was the girl I vented to in my Spanish class, Pam. I would see her at school, but this summer was when I would spend a lot of time getting to know her.

It started because my best friend at the time was dating her, and he would invite me along to go over to her house. I thought that sounded cool, I guess. Anyway, we would go over to her house and the three of us would hang out and talk. I started to take a liking to Pam and so after her and my best friend broke up, I thought now is my chance. Well after a few times meeting at a friend's house and talking on the phone we started going out. She would be my first real girlfriend.

That August it was my sweet 16th birthday party. I just remember what a great experience it was to have a huge party with lots of family and friends. My Dad handed me the keys to a 1977 Chevy Nova for my birthday. I was so excited to get this car. He ended up doing a little work to it and had it painted. Such a cool car. I thought it would be a great idea to drive my girlfriend to school. Right on.

Busted For Pot

I was 16, driving to school, and had a girlfriend. What more would I want? Apparently, I wanted to try to start smoking pot. I know, I know for those of you who do smoke it or do edibles this is not a slam against you so chill out. I don't know why I was wanting to try this but nonetheless I was figuring out a way to get some.

I ended up buying pot from a good friend of mine in my 2nd hour criminal justice class. We were both in the back row of the classroom and we thought no one could see what we were doing. The guy I was buying from had a dollar bill that he used to roll joints and he gave it to me to smell. I thought it smelled pretty good and for whatever reason I thought it would be funny to give that dollar bill to a classmate next to me. He smelled the dollar bill and thought it was disgusting and hunched over his desk. So we made the deal.

As my day was going along in my 4th hour English class, someone from the school office came down to get me and take me to meet with the assistant principal. As I'm waiting for him, I see the classmate that smelled that pot filled dollar bill. Next thing I know the one who sold me the pot is heading out of the assistant principal's office. I was so scared and freaked out. Then the assistant principal comes and gets me and brings me into his office and basically tells me that he knows I did a pot deal in my criminal justice class. He went on to tell me that if I just admit my mistake and I graduate he will take it off my record. I was so nervous and didn't know what to do but eventually I reasoned that it would be better to just admit it and move on. He gave me a 2-week suspension on top of that.

That wasn't the worst part. The worst part is my parents being told what happened. They ended up calling my Mom at her workplace and telling her that she needed to come get me at school. When she got there, she went into the office with the assistant principal to talk about this. I knew I disappointed them and that was the worst feeling in the whole world for me. When my Mom came out of the office, I could tell she was terribly disappointed. It was very awkward going out to the car. She didn't want to leave me home alone, so she took me to her work, and I sat in the car till she finished her day.

My Mom was done working and the ride home was gut wrenching knowing that she would have to break the news to my Dad. When he heard the news, he was very upset as well. I mean I couldn't blame him; I couldn't blame either one of them really. After my parents cooled down, they talked about it and handed down my discipline. They decided that they would take my bass guitar away and I wouldn't be able to play it for the rest of the semester, which would have been about 4 months. I was just glad it wasn't longer. I remember putting my cherry red bass in its case and giving the instrument to my parents for the discipline they were giving me.

This was devastating to me because I was suspended for 2 weeks, and my bass and band were taken away from me for about 4 months. I was surprised how emotional I became about my bass being taken away. I was also surprised how much I would miss playing my bass and writing music with my band. On a side note: All I did throughout high school was going home after school and then go over to Craigs basement and work on music. I would go over there sometimes

5 times a week. I was scared that I would break or jam a finger, so I didn't do sports of any kind except for bowling. I loved that sport.

Identity Revealed

This time away from playing bass was a moment in my life that became a time of rest. In the midst of all the crazy desires to play with the devil, so to speak, and have my mind running a hundred miles an hour thinking about the battle of good vs evil, I actually found rest. Crazy I know, but I was taken out of the storm and was able to find peace. Don't know where it came from, but I wasn't going to complain. I was able to take a deep breath and decompress and clear my thoughts. It was humbling in a way. One thing I learned is that life can put me into a storm of mental distress without me even realizing it. That storm was taking away from me somehow, and there were still waters for a time.

Within these still waters I had time to ponder things. One thing I pondered was, as my bass was absent from my presence, I found out that I missed it. This was a different emotion that I haven't experienced up to that point in my life. I mean I have missed people and such, but not something like this. I wondered why I was missing playing my bass. Maybe it was the physical part of holding the bass and feeling those notes shake the house. I mean who wouldn't miss that...right?

As my mind was being quieted and calmed down, I was able to ponder the concept of what it means to be a bass player. I was realizing that being a bass player was more than a fun hobby. It seemed to be a part of who I was. I would think about what the job of the bass player is. What was the role of the bass player? I didn't really know where these thoughts were coming from or even why it mattered. But nonetheless, it was on my mind.

The Role And Personality

I concluded that the role of a bass player within a band was to outline the harmonic structure of the chord, while playing in time creating the 'pocket' and the groove. I had to ask myself if I was already playing the role of a bass player. This was a great question for me to think about. I mean if I was to be a bass player, I had to understand the role of a bass player and then do my best to stay within that role. I actually started to write all this down so I could remember it. If a bass player has no pocket, then he/she is not doing the job of a bass player. I wondered if I was in the pocket with the bass lines I was playing with Craig and Jack. Thinking about all this was causing me to be critical of my bass playing.

Then I made a list of bass players that I

should analyze their playing. As I listened to my list of bass players, I noticed that the bass lines had different pocket grooves. Some were behind the beat, on the beat and on top of the beat to help create the pocket. This was a huge revelation for me. I also started to hear how some bass lines would play the notes other than the root note of the chord. They would create a ascending or descending bass line within the progression and this would help create direction for the song.

It was definitely great to understand the physical role of a bass player, but then the emotional personality of a bass player took center front stage. The personality of a bass player I came up with this: **Being a foundation for others to build on and being a quiet yet confident leader for the band. In other words, 'looking to the interest of others and not my own.'** I was the foundation of the band. Foundation? That sounded impressive!! I thought about how the foundation of a house must be strong and always there for the house to stand. Everyone would see the house and how beautiful it is but not notice the foundation that it stood on. Same concept with the band. The band has nothing to stand on if the bass player is not being foundational.

I thought about what it meant to be foundational. This is what came to me: **The mindset of being foundational is looking to the interests of others**. I could not draw attention to myself but rather do my part as the bass player and let the other band members shine and make them look good. I was thinking about it and looking to the interests of others was something I was doing for as long as I can remember. It just came natural for me to want to make others happy and see them shine rather than myself. I have always been one to not want to rock the boat, rather to keep the peace.

As I pondered the role and personality of being a bass player, it became crucial for me to understand during this time in my life. Now I had a new approach, and this new way of approaching bass made me feel like I had value, purpose and worth. And because of that, I wanted to be a bass player for life. The emotional and spiritual connection I had with being a bassist became very evident and I realized that being a bass player was who I am. This is when my identity as a bass player took root and started to grow.

My parents ended up letting me start playing my bass again earlier than expected. I was so happy to start playing again after I had this bass player identity revelation. With this new mental approach to bass, it launched me into a confidence which I never had before. I felt as though I could do anything on bass. And in good timing, as my band was also heading into the studio to cut our most difficult and mature songs we wrote together. This mental revelation and studio sessions was the peak point of my bass experience in high school.

Nickname - Beast

The two-week suspension gets done and I have to go back to school. I went back with a quiet attitude and didn't know what to expect from my friends and my teachers. I was hoping this peace I found on my two-week reprieve would continue. It wasn't too long after being back that all the more aggressive thoughts and desire to know occult things was back in my face. For whatever reason I was not bothered with occult-type thoughts when I was suspended, but now it is in my face. It was like it was waiting for me or something, like a switch was turned back on.

As I was getting back in the groove of being back in school, somehow I acquired the nickname of 'The Beast.' A friend said I looked like a beast, and it stuck. Yay me, what a great nickname eh? Not! As friends caught on to that nickname it went from looking like a beast to the satanic reference of me being involved in the occult.

Like I said earlier my favorite album at one time was "The Number of the Beast" by Iron Maiden so it really didn't bother me to joke about being a black mass priest. We would joke about doing a black mass after school, "You bring the cat and I'll bring the knife and meet you at the park". There was a park close to our high school where it was said there would be occult activity and the sacrifice of animals. The joking seemed harmless, but it did keep me thinking about demons and the occult.

'SATAN PREGS'

It's Wintertime now, and my parents wanted to go Up North on an off weekend. My Dad and Mom had a place in Wolverine, Michigan. While growing up we would go there every chance we could. This is something that people in Michigan do. I mean if you live here, you understand there are some things that you do as a Michigander and one of those things is go Up North whenever you can, especially during Christmas and on the holiday weekends.

The winter of my junior year in high school, my parents and myself were heading up to Wolverine for more winter fun. As we were driving up there, I became very tired and decided I should lay down in the van and take a nap. It was a 3-hour drive so I could get in a really nice nap before we got there. We got up to Wolverine and pulled into the driveway of my parents' place. My Dad would always go inside the trailer and light the furnace to warm up the place as my Mom and I would stay in the van. My Mom told me we were there and was trying to get me up to go inside with my Dad. Sometimes I would go in with him but this time for some reason I was unable to get up to go inside with my Dad. My body just felt like it had the life sucked out of it.

My Dad headed into the trailer to light the furnace and I'm closing my eyes because I'm so tired. I'm lying on my back flat at this point and I wanted to turn over to get more comfortable. I go to turn on my side and my body cannot move. I tried moving my arms and they would not move. I tried moving my legs and they would not move. I tried to open my eyes and they would not open. I did not know what was going on. I'm lying flat on my back with my arms crossed over my chest and I literally could not move my body or open my eyes.

I was freaking out and scared. I tried talking and my mouth would not move either. It was like I was talking within my own mind and could not move a muscle literally. I started to scream within my mind, and nothing happened. Then all of a sudden, I heard a soft roar of a fire. It went on for a minute and the roar of the fire started to get louder little by little until it sounded like an inferno.

So here I am laying on my back with my arms folded on my chest, I cannot move a muscle literally and nothing will come out of my mouth, and I hear a fire inferno while all this is going on. I felt as though something was oppressing me and causing me to become trapped within my own mind. I was terrified of what was going on. Within my own mind I was screaming for this to stop but every time I screamed it was met with a louder sound of inferno.

The inferno sound finally met a peak and at that point I had a vision. There was corrugated siding going around my parent's trailer in Wolverine and there was a spot where my Dad would store stuff under the trailer. In this vision I became fixated on this spot and as the inferno fire was raging in my ears, I saw a circle being drawn out over that spot. Then there was a word that started being written out on the top of the circle. As each letter was being written out, I was screaming in my head and trying with all my might to move a muscle. The first letter was an S and when the rest of the letters were written out above the circle, and it spelled the word SATAN. While this was happening, I heard a voice saying "He is mine... he is mine" like someone was trying to claim me. I was terrified because I really felt like I was at the mercy of demons.

Then after the word SATAN was written on the top of the circle there was another word that started to be written out that started on the bottom of the circle. It spelled out what seemed to be a half of a word. P R E G S! Because when it got to the S of the word PREGS there was an abrupt slash that went through the words and circle. When that happened, I was able to open my eyes and my body was released from whatever was keeping it from moving. I was terrified and breathing heavily from this experience when I woke up out of it. I didn't want to startle my mom after I woke up, so I tried not to draw attention to myself. All I know is at that moment I knew that I had some sort of spiritual experience.

After not being able to move a muscle or say anything out of my mouth and experiencing whatever that was, the adrenaline was flowing through my body. I was wide awake. Next thing I know, in a split second, I became extremely tired again and fell back asleep in the same position, on my back with my arms crossed over my chest. And the exact thing happened where I could not move a muscle, nothing could come out of my mouth and voices were trying to claim me. The exact same vision happened the exact same way. After the finger put a slash through the circle with SATAN PREGS written around it, I recognized this finger was something keeping this vision from finishing the word on the bottom. It got to that 'S' and that's when the vision experience abruptly stopped from the finger slash once again.

When I woke the second time again, I didn't want to draw attention to myself, and my Dad was coming out to get us to go inside. I was wide awake. I didn't know what to do or how to act as we went inside the trailer. We just got our stuff inside and I remember feeling anxious like maybe something was going to try and do that again to me. For some reason I had a smile on my face like I was relieved of something. I just felt like there was something in the spirit realm around me. Like it was following me around. I had a hard time getting to sleep that night, but when I did I slept very well.

Of course, this experience was on my mind a lot after it happened. I wanted to talk about it, but I did not know who I should talk to about this. I was taking a psychology class that semester so I thought maybe the psych teacher would have an idea of what I experienced that night. I had an opportunity to share with her what happened. When I was done telling her what happened, she did not have any idea what it was that I experienced. I was kind of bummed out, but I said thank you and kept it to myself.

After that experience Up North with no explanation as to what it was, I became scared to want anything to do with the dark side. That experience freaked me out. When I couldn't move a muscle during that experience, I was vulnerable and scared and if something wanted to do something to me there was no stopping it. I was at their mercy. That was the worst feeling I ever had. I didn’t know if I was going to be taken to hell or killed or what.

After that experience I had to take a moment and try to relax. I had no idea what that was at the time. All I knew is it was evil. Like something you see in a movie. You would think I would be scared enough to not want to listen to all that dark music that I was listening to that I was growing up with. But I would still get those albums and tapes out and listen to them. I would crank them up in my car and roll down the road, and I don't know, what was I thinking?

Senior Year High School

The end of my junior year in high school I was encouraged by my school to figure out what I wanted to do for a career. I thought of all kinds of possibilities. Because of my grades I was kind of limited to what I could choose. I thought about doing marketing or business, but I really wanted to do music. As I thought about it, I decided that I wanted to be a music teacher. And those tests they make you take to find out what careers suit you best confirmed that becoming a music teacher was a good fit for me.

My junior year finished up on a good note. No spiritual experiences, no praying to Satan, no songs beating my door down to bid for my attention. I purposely tried to stay focused on spending time with Pam and jamming with my band. This summer was a transition for the band because Craig and Jack were one grade ahead of me which would make them seniors. It would end up being a beginning to an end. We as a band had a ton of fun that summer jamming together.

As my senior year in high school started, so did the piano lessons to help give me a jump start for college the next year. I always looked forward to the piano lessons because it was like therapy for me. I remember the piano teacher that I had was a soft-spoken, gentle teacher. It was always a time of relaxation. Plus, it gave me vision for what I wanted to do as the lessons started to show me music theory. Just the basics of key signatures and the major scale concept. This would be so helpful when I got to college.

My senior year was on its way, and I did not know what to expect. I mean, my band was realistically coming to an end, and there was really nothing going on with the spiritual battle of my mind. All seemed quiet. Too quiet if you ask me. It ended up being a casual senior year in high school for me. Spending time doing senior year type of stuff- homecoming, time with people I loved, senior yearbook, prom, and planning my open house. It's like I could take a deep breath and rest my mind for a little bit. Just a time of business as usual.

I started to feel uncomfortable about the ongoing conversations of me being referred to the black high priest and my nickname 'The Beast'. I became disinterested in this type of conversation. I purposely passed that title to one of the ones who would joke with me about it. He would say as always, "You bring the knife and I'll bring the cat," and I would say back to him something like, "I am promoting you to high priest and I pass my knife to you." Of course, there was no real knife. He eventually got the idea that I was not wanting to joke about that anymore. He eventually claimed the title and it faded away.

That would end my senior year, along with prom with Pam and a great graduation party. I would transition out of my high school band after one more studio session to record one more song. I was going to go to college and become an adult. I felt as though things were going to be ok.

God Stills The Storm

"He made the storm be still, and the waves of the sea were hushed. Then they were glad that the waters were quiet, and he brought them to their desired haven." Psalms 107:29 ESV

God was doing something without me knowing it was Him doing it. God Almighty does not need my consent to do things in my life. Even though I was not saved and acknowledged Him as Lord, He still came and in His mercy was blessing me with a season of peace. He took me out of the storm that was raging in my mind and put me in still waters. This would allow me a time to think clearly and realize my identity as a bass player. There is no way I could have done this if my life would have kept going the way it was. My mind was reeling with the things going on around me. I didn't even realize how wrapped up my mind was until I was removed from the source of all the chaos.

He removed me from the physical locations of where all this chaos was and that being my high school. He also removed all the demonic influences as well. I did not think about the songs influencing me to be against God or the joking of the black masses after school. Nothing dark entered my mind and I was an open book. This was nothing of my doing because within myself, or my flesh, I wouldn't have been able to do this.

He calmed the storm in me, as Psalm 107:29 says. A storm can sure make you appreciate the peace after it's gone. All of the mental trauma that was being inflicted on me put me in a state of emergency all the time. I couldn't shut my mind down. The Holy Spirit allowed me to get to the point of being mentally out of control and that's when I bought the pot during the second hour Criminal Justice class. I was arrogant enough to do the exchange of goods right in the classroom. When I looked up to the front of the room the teacher was looking right at us. And you read the rest of the story. Who would've thought that being busted for possession of pot would be what initiates this time of still waters.

Looking To The Interest Of Others

I was pushed around pretty easily growing up and I really didn't know how to handle conflict from others. I would go into a mode of making everyone happy so the boat would not get rocked. In doing this I started to create a habit of looking to the interests of others. Was I selfish? Yes. Did I fulfill selfish desires for myself? Yes. But I also did not want to see anyone have to do something they didn't want to. I would sacrifice my wants so others could have what they wanted.

The Holy Spirit was taking something that seemed like a flaw, getting pushed around, and was using that flaw to instill a biblical principle within me. No, Christians are not supposed to be pushed around or be door mats. But we are supposed to consider others better than ourselves and put them first above our own desires. As the Scriptures say *"Do nothing from selfish ambition or conceit, but in humility count others more significant than yourselves. Let each of you look not only to his own interests, but also to the interests of others."* Philippians 2:3-4 ESV

So how does all of this apply to being an aspiring bass player? Well, that's a great question and I'm glad you asked. I came to realize that being a bass player you should not purposely draw attention to yourself. There is a saying in the bass world that says "If no one notices you, when playing with a band, then you have done your job." That's how under the radar a bass player has to be. We are not to draw attention to ourselves. This allows the singer and the guitar player to stick out and do their thing. Even though as a bass player I might want a solo or be center stage, it is just not the way a bass player is to be. We are to do our part and do our job as a bass player and not seek any attention but rather let the singer and guitar player get all the attention. That doesn't mean that the singer and the guitar player are attention seekers but the nature of their role in the band is to be up front and center stage.

In the best interest of the band, I learned what my role was as a bass player. I had to do my part and not 'rock the boat' by what musician's call 'overplaying.' As band members we all have our role to play. Learning to stay within that role is a challenge, especially as a bass player.

Thank you, Holy Spirit, for being patient with me and sowing the seed of looking to the interests of others before I was even born again. Even though I was not saved in high school, God Almighty was planting seeds of His Word without me reading His Word. God Almighty was using what the devil meant to harm for His glory. **The role of the bass player is creating a harmonious groove that is in the pocket by being a foundation for others to stand on**. All of this is possible when the concept of 'looking to the interest of others' is applied.

Battle For My Soul

I have wondered, when I fell into that sleep where I could not move a muscle, what it could have been. I have been told that it was sleep paralysis because it fits the description of what sleep paralysis is. But this was different. This was not just being froze and not being able to speak. There were voices arguing over whose I was. I kept hearing he is mine over and over. Also, the vision I had twice while this was going on. I am convinced that it was a battle of Satan wanting to have more control of me. To this day I wonder what word was being spelled out in the vision while this was going on. All I know is that God stepped in and stopped something from happening. Something was trying to claim me. Either way I am so thankful that God Almighty had mercy on me that night and kept me safe. This would not be the only time it happened to me.

CHAPTER 6 "PRIDE BEFORE THE FALL"

College Years 1987-1990-

Stripped Of My Identity

Things Are Looking Good!

Now I was heading into college, and it just felt different. It was like a new chapter in my life with new beginnings. I would still fixate on the spiritual concept of good and evil, heaven and hell, demons and angels, and trying to wrap my head around it all. I was continuing to experience that there was a spirit realm and that the battle between good and evil was very real.

I started my pursuit as a music major at Mott Community College in Flint, Michigan, with big plans to make music my life and career. At that time, Mott Community College did not have a program for bass so the next best thing for me was classical guitar. Even though I was pursuing classical guitar for my college performance degree, bass stayed as my main instrument of choice.

The band I joined, Surreal, was working hard preparing for the studio to record our first CD *Earth Passages of the Illuminated*. The plan was to finish the CD, pursue record labels, get signed and tour. I have always wanted to rock the stage since I was a young kid. I figured whether I finished my music degree or was signed to a record label it was a win-win for me. I would be doing music for a living either way.

This CD would take a few years to complete but here are some bass highlights of the CD. I would end up writing my first bass composition as we were writing the music for this Surreal CD. It was a simple descending arpeggiated chord progression on my bass with a slow melody in B natural minor. We recorded this song "Tale of Xiab" and at the end of the song, Xiab passes on, so this composition would be his funeral. It is called 'Liquid Eclipse.' I was excited to have it on our CD.

I would also get a funky bass groove I wrote on the album as well, a song called "The Road." This CD would allow me to exhibit many unique bass lines. In another song, I was using a tap harmonic technique. The song "Out of Control" gave a chance for a Steve Harris influenced bass solo using a mixolydian scale. This CD bass-wise covered some many techniques and allowed me to flex my bass muscles you could say. Scott and Ben did a fantastic job forging the project through the flames. Great songwriting and unique lyrics to say the least. I ended up being very proud of this CD, not only the bass work but also as a band, we did something special.

During this time, I also worked at Colonial Lanes Bowling Alley as a bowling alley mechanic. This was my first job, and I loved the work I did. I grew up bowling in leagues and at one point I wanted to be a professional bowler. A bowling alley was a perfect job because I could bowl as much as I wanted. Colonial Lanes also had a really good Billiards room. I bought a pool stick and started spending time learning how to shoot pool. You could say that I would spend all my free time at Colonial Lanes bowling and shooting pool to blow off steam from the pressures of life.

Needless to say, I felt my life was going really well and I couldn't ask for anything more. The band I was in was making a name for itself, school was moving along great, and I was thriving there with my studies. My job was going great and was exactly what I needed to pursue my music and it gave me an outlet to have fun. I felt like I was going where I wanted to go, and no one could stop me from getting there. I had everything I wanted and then some. I was staying 'true to myself' and wasn't letting anything 'repress my freedoms' to fulfill what I wanted, and I was on my way to another 'self-actualization'.

What's Going On

Then one day after a Surreal rehearsal, I noticed that the fingers of my left hand were a little numb. I didn't think much of it and shook it off. As much as I was practicing between both instruments, I thought maybe my hands were a little fatigued. The next few rehearsals I noticed the fingers of my left hand went numb again and this time there was a little pain in my hand. I went and bought some pain cream for my hand thinking that it was muscles and tendons being overworked. Then I took it easy and rested my hand.

A few days later we had a band rehearsal and again twenty minutes into the rehearsal my fingers went numb again. This time not only was my fingers numb but my whole left hand as well. This was very disturbing to me, and I was wondering what was going on. To top that off, when the numbness went away after rehearsal was done my left wrist was in excruciating pain. It was at this point I became very concerned to say the least. I was really hoping that this was nothing serious. After all, I had big music plans for my life, and nothing would stop this from happening.

I remember doing a gig at the Ritz in

Detroit a week later and again my whole left hand became numb two songs into the setlist. I found out that night because I could not take a break between songs like I could during rehearsals that this numbness made it so I could hardly squeeze the neck of my bass. The numbness depleted the strength in my hand. I couldn't even feel my strings that night because my whole hand was so numb. I had no idea where I was going on my bass. It was like I was just throwing my fingers against the neck hoping there would be enough squeeze to get some sort of sound out of my bass. That night I gave up playing the bass lines I wrote for the songs and changed them to something more driving, so I didn't have to move my hands that much. I barely made it through that gig. It was terrible.

I was at a loss of what to say or do after the gig that night. I thought to myself "What is going on? Why is this happening to me?". I thought "Could it get any worse?" Yes, I think it can!! Within a couple weeks numbness and pain were happening in my right hand as well. This was becoming unbearable to handle and something had to give. Now both hands and wrists were going numb and in tremendous pain. I started to feel as though my music career was in jeopardy and going down the tubes really quick. Depression was setting in and I was losing confidence in myself real fast.

I set up a doctor appointment to see what he would have to say. I went to the appointment and after I told him what was going on he casually said that I had carpal tunnel in both my wrists and suggested that I have surgery to fix it. I was speechless at first and it was hard not to burst out in tears right there in his office. I just smiled and said, "Ok Doc, thanks for letting me know what was going on." Then he gave me braces to put on my wrists for when I sleep at night and told me that I could wear them all day long if needed.

When I left his office that day I was devastated, and I just sat in my car afterwards feeling defeated. I couldn't hold back those tears anymore, so I just sat there and cried. After a minute of frustration and cussing out the situation I pulled myself together and I tried to put on a good attitude and follow doctor's orders with the hope that this carpal tunnel would go away.

Within a few days I talked to others about carpal tunnel surgery, and no one had any success stories. The few I talked to said that the surgery was terrible, and the carpal tunnel came back. That was very discouraging. I went and saw a specialist and he said my carpal tunnel was one of the worst he has seen and said surgery is the only way. He explained the risk involved with the surgery and at the time it did not make sense to have the surgery. Besides, I could not afford it.

I decided that I would wear the braces and adapt to playing my bass and guitar while wearing them. I tried playing my bass and that was not too bad, but realistically it wasn't going to work because of the type of bass player I was. A lot of the bass lines were very melodic and required my left wrist to bend a full 90 degrees to play it correctly. The left hand of any classical guitar major has to be at a 90 degree bend all the time so the brace on my left hand was not going to work.

Even though I was frustrated and didn't see the point, I still tried to adapt to playing my bass with the braces on my hands. This was not working at all. Like I said I had to be able to bend my left wrist when I played my instruments. I tried wearing the brace up until rehearsal and then took it off to rehearse only to find my hands still going numb. I was beyond frustrated and becoming more depressed. Now at this point my hands were going numb anytime of the day just out of the blue for no reason. It did not matter if I was playing my bass or not.

The strength in my hands was becoming less and less. Understand this, you have to have strength in your hands to play bass and classical guitar. It just doesn't work if you cannot squeeze the neck of the instrument. And bass requires a lot more strength than classical guitar especially in the left hand. In the bass world some would refer to the left hand as being the 'grip of death' because you would develop tremendous strength in that hand. Even though I was right-handed my left hand was twice as strong as my right. As this carpal tunnel was destroying the strength in my hands and wrists, I found I could barely hold a cup of coffee at times. I had to try and push on even though I was losing all hope to be a musician for life.

Trying To Push On

With all this going on and the fall semester coming up for my sophomore year at Mott, I thought it would be a good idea to talk to my guitar instructor. She had compassion on me and wanted to see me pull through this. I had to do what I had to do to get through this fall semester and hope for a miracle that it would just go away.

I somehow made it to the end of the fall semester, and it was time for jury performances. This is where you perform what you've been working on in private lessons with your instructor and then perform in front of all the instrument instructors of the music department. Then they give you a grade for your performance. This was a requirement to stay in the program. I was nervous and had no confidence in what I was working on in private lessons because of my carpal tunnel.

I was having a hard time getting the music down that my guitar instructor and I were working on in private lessons. I think during my jury performances the instructors had mercy on me, because I did terrible. I remember after the end of my jury performance I ran outside in tears because I was so embarrassed. I had to stop two times during my performance because of numbness and because my knee would not stop shaking due to stress. One of the worst days of my life.

I barely survived the fall semester and made it through only by the grace of God. As the winter semester started, my carpal tunnel was not getting any better. Classical guitar was a hard instrument to master and because of the carpal tunnel I could not do the required studies up to the program's expectations. After talking with my guitar instructor, we decided I should drop out of the music program with the hopes that I would get better. This decision was made with a heavy heart. It was one of the hardest things that I have ever had to do. I felt like the sacrifice I made and the hard work prepping for this program was all for nothing. I was crushed.

I did end up staying in the band Surreal and tried to keep the hope alive that maybe someday I could do music full time despite this medical condition that was ruining my life. I wanted to at least try and see it through with Surreal even though the gigs were gut wrenching. We also had plans to record a CD at the Disc Ltd in Detroit, off Nine Mile Road. Because of the plans to record a CD, I wanted to keep trying.

As we continued doing live gigs, I tried learning how to adapt and take what was given me. When my hand was numb, I would just try and blend in and create a bottom feel. Some nights were not as bad as others as far as the carpal tunnel. It wasn't the most ideal situation, but it was what I had to deal with.

Emotional Toll

This carpal tunnel was stripping me of my bass identity. I saw it as something trying to steal everything that I am. The very essence of who I am. It felt like it was trying to turn me into a different person - like somebody who was not a bass player. What a mess this was becoming, and it started to take an emotional toll on me. The thought of not being a bass player and not doing music was unacceptable in my eyes. I really did not know what I was going to do if I couldn't be a bass player anymore. All this time and effort that went into building my identity was for nothing. That's how I felt anyway. Even though I didn't want to accept it, the pain and numbness in my hands was a constant reminder of reality.

This would send me down a path of depression more and more. I didn't become an alcoholic, but I did keep a steady flow of beer going in me when I was out and about. I just didn't want to think about it and what life would be like without music. I would run scenarios in my head of places I could work and none of them made me feel any better.

One of the things that I realized was that being a musician, for me specifically a bass player, is like being a different breed. Music was a part of my being and woven into my soul. We have heard the saying that 'it's just in my blood.' Well, being a bass player was in my blood, so to speak. To try and quit being a bass player by choice was just not possible. I couldn't quit on myself.

But what I was going through was not my choice. I didn't wish this carpal tunnel on myself. I didn't say "Hello carpal tunnel let's be friends." I mean who would do such a thing? Nobody would. I had dreams and things I wanted to accomplish as a bass player. Tour the world, record in the studio, become one of the greatest bass players known to man. I never asked for this carpal tunnel.

I was emotionally devastated at this point in my life. My dream and identity of being a bass player/musician was being dissolved right in front of my eyes. It was destroying me. I just couldn't believe what was happening to me. I remember feeling hopeless because all of this was out of my control. I was at the mercy of the nature of carpal tunnel or whatever else could be doing this to me.

Suck It Up

I tried to stay strong, but things just were spiraling out of control. I mean how was I supposed to survive without being a bass player or music for that matter. I know it sounds like I'm being a baby by throwing a tantrum and being pouty, but everything was being taken away from me and I didn't know what to do. I felt hopeless. It was going to run its course and destroy my life whether I liked it or not.

Some people said to me "come on man, just suck it up and move on into a different profession, it's life, stop being a baby." That wasn't it though. It wasn't the fact I had to change my career path; it was the fact that all I knew from a young boy was becoming non-existent. I was being forced to become someone I had no idea how to be. I did not know how to act any other way than being a bass player musician. I didn't know how to change my direction in life to become someone else. How was I supposed to re-identify with a different passion in life? Nothing else sparked a passion and drive like music did. I tried sucking it up and I entertained the idea that maybe my current job could be something I could do for the rest of my life, after all I loved the sport of bowling. Then I came to realize that I had no passion to be a bowling alley mechanic and it was just a pass-through job to me. It didn't spark anything in me, and I did not want to make a career out of it.

I would go through a list of other occupations that would be possibilities for me to pursue but I had no desire to pursue any one of them. I thought maybe I could finish a degree in some other field of study, so I started looking into a business or marketing degree. I remembered some friends of mine talking about how those fields of study can make you a lot of money. I had no idea what I would be getting into if I was to pursue these other professions. But it seemed like the right thing to do even though they did not fit my personality.

Throughout all of this, my mind would get worked up and stress me out. It would be nothing for me to sit in my car in the parking lot of Colonial Lanes and get lost in my thoughts about this whole situation. The wear and tear of my mind and all the mental stress took its toll on my mind. The thought patterns that ran through my mind were pinning me down to have a negative outlook of myself. The emotional toll I was trying to endure was overwhelming me.

Purpose, Value And Worth

I started to believe that I was someone without purpose, worth, or value. No purpose, because I believed that I existed to play bass, and with no ability to play bass, meant no purpose. No worth, because now no one will want me to be a part of their project or band because I can't play bass. No value, because everyone who used to have a high opinion of me as a bass player would have to revoke their opinion if I can't play the instrument.

I really tried to hide the carpal tunnel from people. I did not want to have to answer questions all the time as to why I was wearing the braces. I eventually became frustrated and stopped wearing the braces out in public and just tried to wear them at night. This was just embarrassing to me. I felt like such a failure and did not want to talk to anyone about it. I found myself burying these emotions because I did not know how to deal with them.

This feeling of having no purpose, worth, or value would cause me to believe lies about myself. When I was alone, I would confirm these lies and speak out of my mouth "what a failure I am," and "how I will never amount to anything because I don't know how to be anything else." I would curse and just allow anger to come out. I found myself being very anxious all the time and I could not calm my mind down and think straight.

I would also sit and fester and run scenarios through my mind of what was going to happen to me and my future. This would be fuel for my mouth, and I would just let it roll right off my tongue and keep letting myself hear the negativity of the lies over and over. Hearing how I have no purpose, worth, or value over and over. My tongue was poisonous because of what was stirred up in my heart.

Coexisting

"Pride goes before destruction, and a haughty spirit before a fall." Proverbs 16:18 ESV

All three of these identities had to learn to coexist. My bass player identity, my soul identity, and my spiritual identity, had to all make room for each other. So when I graduated high school all three would kick into high gear. One of the three had to dominate and that would be the soul identity. As the spiritual (Christian Identity) was dormant and the bass identity would go along with the soul identity because they both feed off the same thing, that being pride.

There is always a battle for dominance within us all the time. The Apostle Paul talks about this a lot throughout his Epistles. There is the sin nature which is the flesh, and then there is the inner man, or the spirit man, which is our born again spirit. Those two natures will battle for dominance our whole life.

If I was to describe myself, I would say that I was a confident, arrogant musician (bass identity), who did not want to repress anything (soul identity), with a twisted mindset on spirituality from the conflict of Satanic experiences and Christian upbringing (spirit identity).

Pride Does Come Before The Fall

Pride comes before a fall. We have heard this said many, many times, and maybe have actually seen it played out in someone else's life- or maybe this has played out in your own life. You know how it goes- someone around you has everything going for them: good job, nice house, always smiling and in a good mood- you know on top of the world. I think we have all met someone like that.

This is how I felt going into college. I felt like I was on top of the world, and no one could stop me from succeeding in music, and yes...I felt no one could touch me on bass. I saw myself as being above any other bass player around me. So yeah... I was a prideful, arrogant individual. The seed of arrogance that the devil sowed was springing up for sure. As Proverbs 16:18 says, ***"Pride goes before destruction, and a haughty spirit before a fall."***

Let's define a few words before we look at examples from the Scriptures on 'pride coming before a fall.' What does pride mean? Biblically speaking, pride is *having too high an opinion of oneself; arrogant, supercilious.* According to the Merriam Webster Dictionary, a haughty spirit is *blatantly and disdainfully proud : having or showing an attitude of superiority and contempt for people or things perceived to be inferior.* In a nutshell, we could say that pride and a haughty spirit is thinking that you are superior to everyone around you and letting them know that you think you are superior to them.

Where is a good example of this in the Scriptures? There are three passages I want to show you. *"How you are fallen from heaven, O Day Star, son of Dawn! How you are cut down to the ground, you who laid the nations low! You said in your heart, 'I will ascend to heaven; above the stars of God I will set my throne on high; I will sit on the mount of assembly in the far reaches of the north; I will ascend above the heights of the clouds; I will make myself like the Most High.'"* Isaiah 14:12-14 ESV

The phrase 'O Day Star' is referring to Lucifer, which was his name in heaven before he was cast out. This passage by some teachers is considered the five 'I wills' of Satan. In his heart, Lucifer wanted to ascend above God and set up his throne above God and make himself to be like God. Lucifer's opinion of himself was lofty and arrogant and he wanted to be superior to God Almighty. God would not allow this to happen and threw him out of His Presence, casting him out of Heaven.

Jesus even said "And he said to them, *"I saw Satan fall like lightning from heaven."* Luke 10:18 ESV. So we can see the pride that was found in Lucifer's heart caused him to rebel against God ,which then in turn got him casted out and separated from his Creator, God Almighty. Pride came before his fall. Pride always comes before a fall.

We can also see this idea of pride and haughtiness before a fall in the story of Esther, when Haman devised a plan to annihilate the Jewish people. Haman deceived the King to issue a decree to wipe out the Jewish people and sent that decree to all the provinces around them. Haman hated Mordecai because he wouldn't bow down to him. *"And when Haman saw that Mordecai did not bow down or pay homage to him, Haman was filled with fury. But he disdained to lay hands on Mordecai alone. So, as they had made known to him the people of Mordecai, Haman sought to destroy all the Jews, the people of Mordecai, throughout the whole kingdom of Ahasuerus."*Esther 3:5-6 ESV

Haman thought of himself above the Jewish people and wanted them to bow down to him like he was a god. Sound familiar? That's what Lucifer wanted to see happen, and we know what happened to him. As you read the story of Esther, you find out how Haman deceived the king; his pride and haughtiness would lead to his fall. After Haman's deceptive plan to annihilate the Jews was exposed, he ended up being hanged on his own gallows. This story is worth the time to read. Go to the book of Esther in the Old Testament and just read the whole book.

Here is another example of pride before a fall: *"All this came upon King Nebuchadnezzar. At the end of twelve months he was walking on the roof of the royal palace of Babylon, and the king answered and said, "Is not this great Babylon, which I have built by my mighty power as a royal residence and for the glory of my majesty?" While the words were still in the king's mouth, there fell a voice from heaven, "O King Nebuchadnezzar, to you it is spoken: The kingdom has departed from you, and you shall be driven from among men, and your dwelling shall be with the beasts of the field. And you shall be made to eat grass like an ox, and seven periods of time shall pass over you, until you know that the Most High rules the kingdom of men and gives it to whom he will." Immediately the word was fulfilled against Nebuchadnezzar. He was driven from among men and ate grass like an ox, and his body was wet with the dew of heaven till his hair grew as long as eagles' feathers, and his nails were like birds' claws. At the end of the days I, Nebuchadnezzar, lifted my eyes to heaven, and my reason returned to me, and I blessed the Most High, and praised and honored him who lives forever, for his dominion is an everlasting dominion, and his kingdom endures from generation to generation; all the inhabitants of the earth are accounted as nothing, and he does according to his will among the host of heaven and among the inhabitants of the earth; and none can stay his hand or say to him, "What have you done?" At the same time my reason returned to me, and for the glory of my kingdom, my majesty and splendor returned to me. My counselors and my Lords sought me, and I was established in my kingdom, and still more greatness was added to me. Now I, Nebuchadnezzar, praise and extol and honor the King of heaven, for all his works are right and his ways are just; and those who walk in pride he is able to humble."* Daniel 4:28-37 ESV

We can see that there are similarities in all three of these examples of pride coming before a fall. First of all, Lucifer, Haman, and Nebuchadnezzar all wanted recognition as being a god. Lucifer wanted to be like and above God Almighty, Haman wanted the Jews to bow down to him, and Nebuchadnezzar took all the credit for the building of Babylon as if he was a god.

All three were created by Elohim God Almighty, but disregarded the fact that He is God and that He is Sovereign. They all wanted the recognition as being a god. All three had pride and haughtiness in their heart and wanted to be above God or God's created people. They were oppressive and arrogant, wanting the glory and recognition for their accomplishments.

Lucifer was cast out of heaven, and one could conclude that this is where the foundation of pride and arrogance started. He was the first of God's creation to try and go up against Him. Because he hates God's creation, that being the human race, he does everything he can to deceive us and get us to become independent of God which theoretically makes us into our own god.

Haman lost his life because of his pride and

arrogance. He was trying to take the place of God and be like God by oppressing God's people. He developed a hate for the Jewish people because someone, Mordicai, stood up to him and would not bow down to him. There are other stories of God's people not bowing to a man or a man made god. Read Daniel Chapter 3 with Shadrach, Meshach, and Abednego, and Daniel chapter 6 where Daniel was put in the lion's den. All of these men of God would not bow to a man made god. The kings tried to punish them and make an example out of them. Of course, the stories in Daniel show that the punishment backfired, and they would end up giving God Almighty the glory.

Satan even tried to get Jesus to bow to him: *"And the devil took him up and showed him all the kingdoms of the world in a moment of time, and said to him, "To you I will give all this authority and their glory, for it has been delivered to me, and I give it to whom I will. If you, then, will worship me, it will all be yours." And Jesus answered him, "It is written, "'You shall worship the Lord your God, and him only shall you serve.'""* Luke 4:5-8 ESV

Interesting to me is the fact that Lucifer tried to put himself above God Almighty and was casted out of Heaven. In this passage he is trying to tempt Jesus Christ ,the Son of the Living God, by offering all the kingdoms of the world with their authority and glory. Satan was still trying to be above God, his Master, by offering kingdoms that were not his to begin with. Satan will deceive who ever will give him the time of day.

Does God Give And Take Away?

King Nebuchadnezzar wanted to take all the credit for building Babylon. Just like Satan who wants all the attention, be self-serving, and receive all the credit instead of God the Father. Thankfully for Nebuchadnezzar, God humbled him by taking away this kingdom until he recognized his pride and arrogance. Once he realized his wrongdoing and he turned his eyes to God and was restored.

I think Nebuchadnezzar is the one we can relate to the most by today's standards. We are always wanting to take the credit for all of our successes and accomplishments. Well, maybe you don't, but I know that I have a tendency to take the credit. After all, I'm a hard worker and I sacrifice to make things happen...right? Because of those things I should get the credit...uh no! **As a human race we push God out of our lives and do things by being independent of God, and not dependent on God.**

Do you think that Nebuchadnezzar would have recognized his pride and arrogance and the fact he was making himself into a god if God Almighty didn't take away his kingdom to humble him? Do you think that God gives and takes away from us to get our attention today? I think the

Scriptures show us that God in fact does give and take away.

I mean this account of Nebuchadnezzar in the book of Daniel is a perfect scenario. He built something, it became a god, God took it away, while the kingdom was gone he realized his arrogance, turned to God and was restored. Does this scenario sound familiar? I think many of us have a testimony of how God took something away so that we might draw closer to Him and focus more on Him.

A classic example of God giving and taking away is the book of Job, where this Scripture comes from: *"Then Job arose and tore his robe and shaved his head and fell on the ground and worshiped. And he said, "Naked I came from my mother's womb, and naked shall I return. The Lord gave, and the Lord has taken away; blessed be the name of the Lord.""* Job 1:20-21 ESV When Job said this, he just got news that he lost his livelihood, and his children were killed as well. All this news came at the same time. If you read before that you find that Satan is the one who destroys Jobs' life, but it was God who allowed it. God is sovereign. When Job says that God gave, and God takes away, he is recognizing God's sovereignty. Read the first few chapters of Job to let this sink in.

I have spent a lot of time on the idea that 'God is sovereign' to stay this: God allowed me to develop as a bass player and create this identity within me. He ***gave*** me this talent on the bass guitar even though I wasn't saved. I made bass and music into a god in my life and became prideful and very arrogant. God allowed Satan to bring carpal tunnel on me. I'll say that again - God allowed Satan to bring carpal tunnel on me. The carpal tunnel was what God chose to use to ***take away*** this talent of being a bass player. This was the beginning of God drawing me to His Love, Mercy and Grace, without me even realizing it.

CHAPTER 7
"TRUTH REVEALED"

Spring 1991

Heaven And Hell

About a year goes by and my band Surreal is in the studio and I'm still dealing with this identity-crisis, and seeing my music career going down the tubes because of carpal tunnel. I was barely making it through the studio sessions because the pain and numbness were still evidently present. But the Surreal CD was moving along, even though all this was going on.

This carpal tunnel was depressing me bad, so I was also spending all my spare time at the Colonial Lanes bar. As I sat there having a beer one night, I started having some unexpected thoughts come to my mind. For whatever reason, I started thinking about the concept of Heaven and Hell. I busted out with a chuckle as I was sipping my beer and I thought to myself this is something I haven't thought about in a long time. I wondered where this was coming from.

I entertained this thought of Heaven and Hell for a minute while sitting at the bar, had some fun with it, and then put it to rest. A few minutes later it pops into my mind again. I asked myself what is up with this and why am I thinking about it again. I mean, I was trying to wallow in self-pity and fester over the fact that my music dream was barely alive, soon to be dead and gone. But this thought of Heaven and Hell just wouldn't go away. I was like 'whatever' and I just went with the flow, entertaining it that night, thinking to myself, 'why not?'

The next day I get up and start getting ready for work and wouldn't you know it, you guessed it, this Heaven and Hell concept starts coming in my mind again. I took a deep breath and I really felt like I had to give this some attention. Again, I questioned why I was thinking about it so much out of the blue. It's not like I was watching movies or listening to the music I grew up with to trigger this thought pattern. I was surprised that this would go on for a few days.

Which One? The Conversation Begins

Then one day, for whatever reason, I started thinking about this concept of Heaven or Hell a little differently. It was like there was a gut feeling and a voice in my head talking to me about this subject. This of course was nothing abnormal for me. Nonetheless, questions were asked inside my mind- and this is what they were: Which one would I go to when I die? Heaven? Or Hell? Which one would I take up residence when I am thrusted into eternity? Heaven? Or Hell? Which one is my destiny as of this day, right now, as we speak? I paused and took a step back.

I never thought about this before. I mean, I've pondered what heaven could be like and I've even pondered what hell could be like. But I never pondered which one I might end up going to after I physically pass on. I tried to come up with an answer right away, but I couldn't. I tried to say I was going to heaven, but I couldn't even say that with confidence and assurance. I asked myself this: if I could not confidently say that my destination was heaven does that mean my destination would be hell? I wasn't even sure about that either. The question still remained, heaven? Or hell? Which one? I had no idea, so my answer was- I don't know.

That was very frustrating having to admit that I didn't know something. I had no idea what to even gauge as to whether I was heaven or hell bound. And because I had no idea, I felt lost and uneasy. What does it mean now that I realize that my eternal destination is uncertain? I didn't know what to do with all this and it would weigh heavy on my soul for days to come.

Three Views Of Hell/Devil

As this newfound concept of eternal uncertainty would not leave my thought pattern, I became nervous and paranoid about putting myself in a position of dying. I found myself being more careful about everything around me. During this time a co-worker was killed in a car accident. He was only a few years older than me. This really freaked me out and made me realize that I could die at any moment in my life. I reasoned that time is not guaranteed in life even at 21 years old. I became more uneasy about all of this.

I really wanted to get a serious understanding of what hell is. I found myself reflecting on what I have come to perceive hell to be. There were so many seeds that were planted in me growing up as to what hell could be. I took the time to ponder this concept. I thought if you are gonna focus on hell you have to include the devil. I saw hell as being the devil's kingdom so you can't have one without the other.

When I focused on the concept of hell, I was reminded of growing up and how I perceived hell as being a joke. I sure did not take it serious at all. As I got older and allowed my flesh to conform to the patterns of this world it became harder to take it seriously. When I would be out bowling or shooting pool and drinking, I coined the catch phrase "drink up, and I'll see you in hell." It would get a good laugh among friends but as I thought about it now it just didn't feel right.

In high school I thought of the devil as someone who understood me and had my best interests at hand. I felt as though the devil, and I were a team, and we would take on the verbal persecution from upper authorities of teachers and religious leaders making a big deal of how rock-n-roll is a bad influence on me. I really felt as though the religious people were trying to brainwash me and wanted me to conform to their way of thinking. I felt as though I had to pick a side. Which team I would want to be on. Kinda like picking teams as a kid when playing football or something. I found myself thinking that hell was the team to be on because it seemed like I was always being bullied by the upper authorities in my life.

As I thought about these views of hell and the devil. something inside me told me that these views were wrong. What I thought was right was now being challenged by something in my gut. Now, what I thought was wrong was starting to seem right. This was not making sense to me. This gut feeling was muddying the waters on these views that were developed in me from a child. Was hell really a joke? Was the devil really someone I wanted to defend?

Then I realized that those songs I grew up

singing all the time developed these views on hell and the devil over the course of my upbringing. I would listen to them over and over and over and wear those records out. Especially the song "Highway to Hell." I came to this conclusion: that song alone is responsible for developing the majority of my overall views of hell and the devil. This gut feeling continued challenging me to see the truth of what I believed to be good and what I believed to be bad.

Fear Is Developed

After contemplating these views of hell and the devil I had to admit that maybe hell was a possible reality of what I was taught in church and not rock music. I really wanted to figure this out because it was driving me crazy. I paused and thought to myself that I would start with what I remember from my upbringing in the church. I had a general understanding that there was a God and a devil. One was in heaven, and one was in hell, one was good, and one was bad. That was a good place to start.

Just the thought of hell being a possible reality was enough to develop a fear inside me. This fear really started to get my mind thinking. Maybe I was hell bound. The anxiety, and of not knowing and having uncertainty of what to expect when I die, was intensifying. I questioned what would send me to hell. Then I questioned what would save me from hell. This was so confusing. Nothing was making sense. I concluded that if I didn't know what would keep me out of hell or send me there, then I can assume I am hell bound. I thought to myself, 'Is any of this true?' I mean I joked about hell for years and felt like the devil was a friend and not an enemy and it never seemed like something of reality. But something inside of me kept bringing all this up to the forefront of my mind and would not let it go away. I would say it out loud several times that I was hell-bound. I closed my eyes and took a deep breath. I was having a hard time accepting this reality because I questioned as to whether heaven and hell are even real. But this uneasy feeling and this fear inside me was undeniable. Why would I feel this way if it wasn't real?

Knowing how I am though, I had to figure this out whether it was a real thing or not. With that said, in my eyes I saw this 'hell-bound' revelation as a problem, and there are always solutions for every problem. Therefore, there had to be a solution to this problem. There had to be something I could do or not do to keep me from going there. I started to talk myself into the idea that I can find this solution. I thought, I don't have to go to hell, I can fix this, I just need to put together a logical plan and figure this out, because there has to be something to keep me from being hell bound. Even though fear was struck inside of me, I wasn't fully convinced that any of this was real. I had to create a hypothetical scenario to exhaust the possibilities. With that in mind I started to make a list to figure out what I was missing.

What Is Hell?

I felt pretty confident I could figure this out even though I wasn't convinced hell was real, or heaven for that matter. I believed that this way I could have peace of mind. I thought I would start with figuring out what hell really is. All those other questions and running scenarios in my head lead me to ask the question, 'what is hell?' In my confirmation classes at Holy Cross Lutheran Church, I was taught that hell is not a good place. That it is a place of weeping and gnashing of teeth, a place of pain and suffering, where the fire is never quenched, and the worm never dies. Oh my, I don't want to go there!

As I was running scenarios through my mind as if hell was real, this came to me- ***Hell is the complete separation from God's presence.*** Whoa... I had to let this sink in for a minute. I thought, "Is this true? Is Hell the separation from God's presence?" Something inside me said "Yes." When I thought about hell as a means of separation, I acquired a different perspective. All of a sudden, this whole thing started to feel real. I started to imagine what it would be like in hell. The screams, torture, fire, and not to mention the demons who I always imagined to be ruthless and merciless monsters. This would continue to stoke the flames of fear already inside me.

This fear was bringing out of me real concerns. Deep down inside me I knew heaven and hell were real. There was just an unknowing conviction of this reality. I just wasn't convinced. I had too many questions without answers. And because of these questions it kept me in this place of doubt. **Doubt and fear would keep me in a place of confusion because I wasn't convinced as to what to believe.**

Just using common sense about the things, I was remembering from Sunday school and church were making the side of the devil unappealing. If what I remembered is true, then I don't want to be there when I die. Something in my gut continued being persistent and telling me that I want to be on God's side. I thought if all this is real then how? How am I supposed to be on God's side? What is the formula? Do I have to do something? Say something? What do I have to do?

The logic that cycled through my head was this: If hell is real, then hell is separation from God, and I will go to hell if I die. To be on God's side, what do I have to do? Over and over, I would fester on the cycle of that thought process. When I got to the end of the cycle and wondered 'what do I have to do' I always had the same answer...I don't know. I tried to take a break from thinking about this for a few days- I had a headache trying to figure this out.

I Am A Sinner?

A few days went by, and my mind was rested, and I just happened to be in a good mood. Even though all this was confusing I was still determined to figure out how to be on God's side and gain access to heaven. I went and bought a pack of legal pads and a bag of my favorite pens, and I was ready to start writing down what I knew.

After asking all those questions and tweaking the questions and trying to use some sort of logic I came to this conclusion: I am separated from God and hell bound. I needed to somehow figure out how to get on God's side. That's where I was at with this whole thing. Plain and simple. I am the type who has to exhaust many options and try and look at every angle.

I got to thinking about what it takes to be on God's side. How do I get there? That was my question to focus on. The thought process of thinking about hell and the devil and what it is like, being separated from God, being hell-bound, and then dealing with the fear created because of it, and still having doubts, was a lot to process. I wanted to take a break from that and think about how to get on God's side.

The first thing I thought of was that there had to be something that was stopping me from knowing how to get right with God. I looked at what I wrote down and went through the list: Is this real, I am separated from God, I am hell bound, and how to get on God's side. I went back through this list a few times and then I stopped at 'I am separated from God.' It was like this phrase jumped off the page. I couldn't take my eyes off it, and I couldn't get it out of my head.

I thought about this for a minute and then said it out loud "I am separated from God." Then I thought "If I am separated from God then what is separating me from God? What is the one thing that is separating me from God?" I had to think about that for a minute. This would end up being the most important question in this whole process. As I thought about it, and I had one of those conversations with myself of possibilities going through a process of elimination. Of course, I made a list so I could keep track of what I was thinking out loud in this conversation with myself. Then, as I got myself worked up into a frenzy doing this, something caught my attention and in a gentle voice I heard 'my sin.' I stopped, and there was this moment of 'did I hear that right?' I didn't know where this came from but, as I thought about this it made sense. I then realized what was separating me from God...it was ***my sin***.

There it is! Therein lies the problem. Ding!

Ding! Ding! My sin was causing me to be separated from God, which in turn would make me not right with God. It was like a light bulb went off inside my mind. What a moment this was in my life! I was actually relieved that this revelation came to me. Most people, when they think of sin in their life get defensive, but I actually had a sense of freedom knowing that sin was the problem. I must have remembered this concept from confirmation classes, Easter service, or even the part of the Sunday service where Lutherans confess their sins:

> *Most merciful God, we confess that we are by nature sinful and unclean. We have sinned against You in thought, word, and deed, by what we have done and by what we have left undone. We have not loved You with our whole heart; we have not loved our neighbors as ourselves. We justly deserve Your present and eternal punishment. For the sake of Your Son, Jesus Christ, have mercy on us. Forgive us, renew us, and lead us, so that we may delight in Your will and walk in Your ways to the glory of Your holy name. Amen.*

It was like I had knowledge of this from reciting it every time I was at church, but now I understood it, and it made sense. I reasoned that I had to start with understanding sin. Understanding sin would then help me understand how to get right with God. That was my thinking anyway.

I thought about the question 'What is sin?' My initial answer was 'I don't know.' As I thought about that question more, I was led to think about what I learned in confirmation classes. What I remembered was the Ten Commandments. I remember in class learning that the Ten Commandments were the standard to live by and if you broke any commandment you are sinning. I started to feel better about all this because things started to make more sense.

I thought 'Alright, I'm not a bad person, so there should not be too much sin in my life.' I decided I should examine myself against the Ten Commandments that I could remember. I asked myself if I ever killed anyone- and the answer was no. Ok, I'm starting out good. Then I asked myself if I ever lied, hmmm, I had to say that I have lied before. I am one for two. Then I asked myself if I ever committed adultery, and based on how I understood it I had to say yes. Ok now I'm one for three.

As I went through the other commandments, I realized that I have sinned and there was no denying it. I was a Law breaker and couldn't just sweep it under the rug. Sin was at every stop for me. I was saturated with sin. I just logically came to the conclusion that ***I am a sinner***, which then means I am ***separated from God***, which would mean that I am ***going to hell when I die.*** Hell was going from "what if it exists" to "this is a reality, and it does exist." Not a comforting thought at all, but the truth about myself in relation to sin had to be revealed.

The Role Of The Holy Spirit

"And when he comes, he will convict the world concerning sin and righteousness and judgment: concerning sin, because they do not believe in me; concerning righteousness, because I go to the Father, and you will see me no longer; concerning judgment, because the ruler of this world is judged." John 16:8-11 ESV

Does the Holy Spirit work in the lives of unbelievers? Absolutely yes! The Holy Spirit plays such a huge role in the lives of both the believer and the unbeliever. **He abides in the hearts of the believer and prepares the hearts of the unbeliever.** To the believer He is Counselor, Helper, the Mind of Christ, Breath of Life, Spirit of Truth and bears witness with a believer's spirit. To the unbeliever He is the plowman who tills the soil of their heart that the implanted Word may take root and He is the one who lifts the blinders off the eyes of those who do not see the truth.

I was having a hard time seeing the truth. I couldn't understand it because I didn't have the Holy Spirit dwelling inside of me. The Holy Spirit was taking me down a path to understand the truth by first prompting me through 'gut feelings.'

He would stay consistent and wouldn't let up on me at all. Even though it created a lot of stress to realize I am a sinner it had to be done. I would never have realized that I needed Christ Jesus as my Savior unless I first recognized that I was a sinner. That's what the Holy Spirit was doing during this time in my life. He was helping me understand that I was lost without Christ Jesus.

As the Holy Spirit was putting thoughts into my mind and giving me 'gut feelings' it would help me through the logical process. Not everyone will go through the same logical thought patterns as I did, but there is a logical process. The Holy Spirit knew exactly what I needed to think through to get me to the point of realizing I am a sinner. That I am lost and dead in my sin and that I need a Savior.

The Holy Spirit was convicting me of my sin. Conviction of sin is one of the roles of the Holy Spirit *"And when he comes, he will convict the world concerning sin and righteousness and judgment: concerning sin, because they do not believe in me;"*John 16:8-9 ESV He was not convicting me of my sinful behavior but rather the fact that I was a sinful being and did not believe in Christ Jesus with my heart. And because of this I was separated from God and needed a Savior to reconcile me and redeem me from my sin.

The Holy Spirit didn't convict me for having another beer, lighting up another cigarette, or trying to fulfill the flesh. No, He revealed the truth that I am a sinner and need Christ Jesus to save me from my sin. At this time in my life, I didn't understand what Christ crucified really did by dying on the cross, being buried and resurrected on the third day. But the Holy Spirit was patient, steadfast and did not give up on me.

This revelation of realizing I am a sinner would be the beginning of pointing me to the truth of Christ Jesus and His saving power and grace. What I am telling you right now is the beginning to understanding the Gospel. **If you do not believe that you are a sinner, then you will not understand the need for a Savior. Unbelieving sinners see no need for a Savior and justify their actions with their own pride and humanist philosophies.**

Sin Separates- We Need A Savior

Every human being on the planet-
past, present, and future, are born with a sin nature. Which means we will sin naturally and not desire to obey God and His Word. Sin separates us from God. *"But your iniquities have separated you from your God; your sins have hidden his face from you, so that he will not hear."* Isaiah 59:2 NIV The Bible says that our spirit is dead in sin (Ephesians 2:1) and our heart is deceitful (Jeremiah 17:9). Adam and Eve brought sin into the world *"Therefore, just as sin came into the world through*

one man, and death through sin, and so death spread to all men because all sinned—" Romans 5:12 ESV

Let's take a look in the Scriptures of the account of how sin entered into the world, as Paul says in Romans 5:12: *"Now the serpent was more crafty than any other beast of the field that the Lord God had made. He said to the woman, "Did God actually say, 'You shall not eat of any tree in the garden'?" And the woman said to the serpent, "We may eat of the fruit of the trees in the garden, but God said, 'You shall not eat of the fruit of the tree that is in the midst of the garden, neither shall you touch it, lest you die.'" But the serpent said to the woman, "You will not surely die. For God knows that when you eat of it your eyes will be opened, and you will be like God, knowing good and evil." So when the woman saw that the tree was good for food, and that it was a delight to the eyes, and that the tree was to be desired to make one wise, she took off its fruit and ate, and she also gave some to her husband who was with her, and he ate."* Genesis 3:1-6 ESV

Let us put Genesis 3:1-6 into perspective. Here is Adam and Eve enjoying the creation of Elohim, when Eve is faced with something she has never had to face. Here comes a crafty serpent with a slick tongue to deceive her. Before woman was created, Adam was given the command from God Almighty to not eat of the tree of the knowledge of good and evil. *"And the Lord God commanded the man, "You are free to eat from any tree in the garden; but you must not eat* *from the tree of the knowledge of good and evil, for when you eat from it you will certainly die.""*Genesis 2:16-17 NIV

So Adam knew what God commanded as the one thing he was supposed to refrain from doing. The Scriptures tell us that Eve had this knowledge as well. I would speculate that Adam explained everything to Eve, and that God had told him before she was created. It is evident because during the conversation with the serpent she quotes what God commanded her. They both had knowledge of God's command and even the serpent had knowledge of God's command.

When we look at what the serpent does, he first creates doubt in God's command by saying 'You will not surely die.' He was reasoning with Eve about God's command. This created a breakdown of trust in what God said was ok to do and what was not ok to do. After the serpent created doubt in God's command, the serpent then tempts her with the idea of being like God and not being content with being God's creation, but instead she could now be at the same level as God.

Does this sound familiar as the reason the devil was cast out of heaven? Lucifer wanted to be like God, *"How you have fallen from heaven, morning star, son of the dawn! You have been cast down to the earth, you who once laid low the nations! You said in your heart, "I will ascend to the heavens; I will raise my throne above the stars of God; I will sit enthroned on the mount of assembly, on the utmost heights of Mount Zaphon. I will ascend above the tops of the clouds; I will make myself like the Most High."* "Isaiah 14:12-14 NIV

Being like God was the desire that was conceived inside of Eve's heart. *"When the woman saw that the fruit of the tree was good for food and pleasing to the eye, and also desirable for gaining wisdom, she took some and ate it. She also gave some to her husband, who was with her, and he ate it."* Genesis 3:6 NIV The serpent created physical desire to eat it, a soul type desire to want it, and a spiritual desire to have wisdom. She was deceived into thinking that it was ok to disobey God's command of 'Do not eat the fruit of the tree of the knowledge of good and evil, or even touch it.' And yes, she gave some to her husband who was with her, and he did nothing to stop it.

Because Adam and Eve disobeyed God, all of mankind fell into sin (Romans 5:12). At that point mankind inherited the sinful nature of the world. And there were consequences for their action of this one act of disobedience. The major consequence of inheriting the sinful nature is separation from God. Sin cannot be in the presence of God at all because of His Holiness. God had to banish Adam and Eve from the Garden of Eden or in other words God had to separate Himself from the inherited sin of Adam and Eve.

Holy Spirit

The Holy Spirit was getting me to take the first step of a saving knowledge of Christ Jesus by convicting me of my sin. I just have to say, that it wasn't a guilt-ridden conviction of sin. It was more a 'I am separated from God' type of conviction. I tell you right now, the role of the Holy Spirit convicting us is crucial to walk with God. Whether it be on the road to salvation, or if you're saved then fall into sin. Either way, you are separated or separating yourself from God the Father.

Do you know the story of David in the Bible? David was a man of God, and he was anointed king over God's people. Then he was tempted by watching Bathsheba bath outside. We know the story: he lays with her, gets her pregnant, then tries to cover it up by bringing her husband Uriah back from war to have him lay with her. It would be perceived that she became pregnant by Uriah. Uriah doesn't lay with her though and ends up going back to war and David tells his generals to put him on the front lines where Uriah ends up being killed in the line of duty.

This is an example of the sinful nature at work. The sinful nature will cause us to sin because it wants to disobey God's commands. Obviously, David is on a roll of sinful actions: lying, adultery, murder, coveting a man's wife. Then his pride blinds him to not see his sin and he goes on with his life with this stain of sin on his hands and a pregnant mistress, who he eventually married. He knows better but will still not acknowledge his sin and reconcile to God. Then God sends a prophet Nathan to confront David.

"The Lord sent Nathan to David. When he came to him, he said, "There were two men in a certain town, one rich and the other poor. The rich man had a very large number of sheep and cattle, but the poor man had nothing except one little ewe lamb he had bought. He raised it, and it grew up with him and his children. It shared his food, drank from his cup and even slept in his arms. It was like a daughter to him. "Now a traveler came to the rich man, but the rich man refrained from taking one of his own sheep or cattle to prepare a meal for the traveler who had come to him. Instead, he took the ewe lamb that belonged to the poor man and prepared it for the one who had come to him." David burned with anger against the man and said to Nathan, "As surely as the Lord lives, the man who did this must die! He must pay for that lamb four times over, because he did such a thing and had no pity." Then Nathan said to David, "You are the man! This is what the Lord, the God of Israel, says: 'I anointed you king over Israel, and I delivered you from the hand of Saul. I gave your master's house to you, and your master's wives into your arms. I gave you all Israel and Judah. And if all this had been too little, I would have given you even more. Why did you despise the word of the Lord by doing what is evil in his eyes? You struck

down Uriah the Hittite with the sword and took his wife to be your own. You killed him with the sword of the Ammonites. Now, therefore, the sword will never depart from your house, because you despised me and took the wife of Uriah the Hittite to be your own.' "This is what the Lord says: 'Out of your own household I am going to bring calamity on you. Before your very eyes I will take your wives and give them to one who is close to you, and he will sleep with your wives in broad daylight. You did it in secret, but I will do this thing in broad daylight before all Israel.' " Then David said to Nathan, "I have sinned against the Lord." Nathan replied, "The Lord has taken away your sin. You are not going to die. But because by doing this you have shown utter contempt for the Lord, the son born to you will die."" 2 Samuel 12:1-14 NIV

We see a process here. David sinned, David tried to cover up his sin, David did not acknowledge his sin. Then, Nathan confronts David and shows him his wrongdoing. It wasn't until that time that David finally acknowledged his sin, as we see in verse 13: "I have sinned against the Lord." Once he acknowledges his sin, he is forgiven. David still had to accept the consequence of his action of sin, which was the death of his son from Bathsheba.

Now, knowing this about David, you would think that God would take him out of His plan of salvation and move the bloodline of Christ Jesus through someone else. But, David was the 'apple in

God's eye'. *"Keep me as the apple of your eye; hide me in the shadow of your wings,"* Psalm 17:8 ESV

Just like David, I sinned. Every one of us commits sin. I was blinded by the world's pride and would justify my sin. I just did what I wanted and if it felt good, I would do it. I didn't know any better. Then I would justify my sin because I was ignorant to God's Word. As human beings we justify our sin because we do not want to admit that we are wrong about something. For me, it was like a stubborn pride not wanting to give up its right to sin, justified actions of sin.

Then the Holy Spirit convicted me of my sin and showed me how it separates me from God the Father. And because of that, I needed a Savior to save me from my justified sin. This would end up being the most important concept to understand in this journey I was on. It's not that I was a bad person, it was simply the fact that my sin was keeping me from being in God's presence. Then I thought what comes next. I really did not know what came next. What was I supposed to do now?

I was scared and my doubts created fear in me. It was because of the unknown that I became scared. The unknown of my eternal destiny and this knowing in my gut that I was separated from my Creator. I realized that I didn't like being in a place of not knowing. I decided that I would dedicate time and effort into figuring this out. There had to be a solution to the problem, right? I would start to try and find salvation on my own. It was the only thing that made sense to me at the time.

CHAPTER 8 "NOT MY UNDERSTANDING"

Figure Things Out

Just Get Rid Of It - Go To Church

Sin just seemed like a dirty word- or like a disease of sorts. I asked the question: how was I supposed to get rid of sin? As I thought about it, I realized I had no idea! I desperately thought that maybe I could just crumple it up and throw it away. Or maybe drain it out of my being. Or even take a bath and scrub it off me. Of course, I'm kidding on all that. But I was trying to figure out what to do.

Even though I was glad I was convicted by the Holy Spirit there was more stress put on me by this new revelation that I am a sinner destined to hell. Or maybe it was something I knew all along and it was a revived revelation. Either way, it caused me stress. When I stress out, I make a list of what the stress is to try and identify the cause of the stress. This is what I came up with: Carpal tunnel stealing my identity, leading to depression which caused me to want to drink more, everything in my life was up in the air like there was no sense of direction. And now, there is this to deal with as well- am I going to hell?

One might say “Dude, what's the big deal? Just go to church and ask a Pastor or someone like that to take care of this for you- isn’t that what church is for?” At first that thought did not cross my mind, then I thought “that just might work, maybe I should ask a Pastor.” I started to ponder all the churches I could set an appointment with in my hometown to talk to their Pastor. I thought that trying to talk to the Pastor at the church I grew up at would be a bad idea. Too much familiarity. I assumed there would be criticism and chastisement. In my mind, I didn’t want to face the music.

I was too embarrassed to step foot into any church for that matter, because I felt like all of them, including the church I grew up at, would condemn me. My thought was I haven’t been to church in forever and I was living a heathen lifestyle. This made me feel vulnerable and uncomfortable. I honestly believed that I had to get cleaned up, purged of sin, before I could go talk to a Pastor or someone. I figured that's what they would tell me to go do, "Go get cleaned up Mike, then come talk to me." I imagined the frown of disapproval on their faces and the finger pointing to the door to go and stop living a heathen lifestyle.

I also saw the church as a representation of a critical authority telling me what to do and how to act. I didn't take correction very well. I developed a rebellious attitude because I thought that the church was out to repress my freedoms. Even though I didn't identify with secular humanism, I shared a lot of their views and ideas. This was one of them. I wanted to do what I wanted, when I wanted, and not have to deal with anyone telling me I was wrong for doing it.

Even if I did go to church at that time in my life it wouldn't have mattered. I wouldn't have admitted that I was a sinner, separated from God, and destined to hell. I mean I admitted it to myself, but I didn't want to admit it to a Pastor. That would mean that I would have to admit that the church was right about something. Besides, I wanted to do this on my own. Boy, my pride would be the death of me for sure. I knew even at that time in my life that pride was keeping me from knowing the truth. But I did nothing about it. In my mind I did not need any help to figure this out. There was a solution out there and I was determined to find it.

One Pool Session- Afterlife?

It was my usual Friday night plans to go out and shot pool at Colonial Lanes. Made some phone calls to try and find someone to come and hang out with me and shoot some pool but for some reason everyone was busy that night. But because I loved the game of pool, I went by myself. About fifteen minutes into shooting pool, I of course got to thinking about this hell dilemma again. No one was around to distract me, so my mind just started to wander. This is what came to my mind that night.

Even though my gut was telling me that heaven and hell are very real this is what I started to think about: maybe heaven and hell are not real after all, and all this emotion of fear is being spent for no reason. You might be saying, "Dude, you just said that Heaven and hell are real so how can you say they may not be real?" Welcome to my world. I would always go back and forth on this concept, and I could never feel 100% that either one existed. Even growing up I would question my Sunday school teacher.

As I shot pool that night, I thought that maybe heaven and hell could be seen through the lens of the afterlife. My thought was that heaven and hell are two concepts that would exist after my physical death. I could relate to the idea of the afterlife because it seemed to be a less harsh and universal word for life after death for Christianity and many religions. It seemed that every religion had its own destination in the afterlife different, yet similar, in each one.

Even though I could relate to the idea of the afterlife, it was a hard concept to grasp. To think that somehow we can live beyond this life after we die. By definition, afterlife is existence in which the essential part of an individual's identity or their stream of consciousness continues to live after the death of their physical body. So this was mind blowing to think about how we could live on in this conscious state of mind.

That night my mind would ponder the idea of consciousness living on past physical death. I thought, how is this even possible? I thought if this is possible then there has to be something inside of me that would live on, that being my conscious state of mind. There had to be something to house this conscious state of mind-which is my will and emotions: my thinking. I wondered what that would look like. Would it be an invisible me with this consciousness? Or maybe some kind of celestial body similar to what we already have. Who knows but needless to say this was becoming an interesting night.

Satan Confirms God's Existence

I was still there shooting pool, and being reminded of the things I have already been through up to that point in my life. I thought about all the events and things I did and saw and thought about growing up through high school. The music I listened to was influential and at one point I prayed to the devil, and I wanted to be a witch.

But the one experience that I cannot forget is the SATAN PREGS experience I had up north when I believed that Satan was trying to take over my soul. That experience was a dark one interacting with the kingdom of Satan. There were voices in my head trying to claim me when I was physically frozen and mute, twice! It was like there was a war for my soul that night. That's the only way I could interpret it. It was like Satan was trying to take me over and have control of me. When the finger stopped writing in my vision abruptly it was like the striking of a sword. Like something was breaking the bondage that was physically freezing me and making me mute.

Sometimes experience has to override facts. I didn't have the facts but I had the experience. This experience continued to confirm that the spirit realm was one hundred percent real. After that experience I remember just looking at things differently. I was more and more comfortable with the spirit realm after that night. As that night went on, I could actually see that there was something around me in the spirit realm. It was kind of freaky at first but after a while I would become accustomed to this kind of thing.

I would think about the SATAN PREGS experience and the other other experiences I had growing up. I came to realize that there were just too many things that I experienced where I could not not deny anymore that God and Satan existed. **These experiences of the occult type of activity and dark spiritual encounters showed me that Satan existed and, in my mind, if he existed then God had to be real as well.**

This was an important night because it settled the idea that God and Satan exist, and heaven and hell are real destinations. Too many spiritual experiences to say otherwise. I knew deep down all this was true, I just had to go through the process of thinking it through. When this revelation came to me that night I felt as though a battle was won inside myself. Like the fighting of both sides ceased. All I know, is I was physically exhausted, and I could physically feel my body relax. I felt as though the rough waters became still waters. I took a deep breath in and out a few times. Took a minute to enjoy this peace of mind and then went back to playing pool and kept to myself the rest of the night.

Who Is God?

After that night I knew that my next move was to get on God's side and get off the devil's side. 'To get right with God' is what came to my mind. I needed to figure out how to be heaven bound and not hell bound. My thought was I wanted to get to know the captain of God's team. That being God Himself. I then asked the question who is God? I wanted to understand who He is. He seemed so big and far away. But at the same time, He seemed so close. Was He someone I could get to know, even though I could not see Him or touch Him?

I remembered there was a lot about God in the Old Testament stories I learned from Sunday school. I thought I would start there. I have to be honest, all that stuff I learned in the Bible when I was growing up just seemed hard to believe. I mean those stories in the Old Testament were like a fiction movie to me. The story of Creation, the Great Flood and Noah's Ark, the story of Joseph, Moses and the parting of the Red Sea, David and Goliath, Daniel and the Lion's Den, etc.

All those stories seem to have the concept of the impossible becoming possible, and that is all I remembered. I still wasn't able to get anything out remembering those stories except that God did some miraculous things. It was like I was a spectator at a sporting event. I could tell you about the game but didn't know anyone who was playing the game.

Get Right With God

As I was thinking about who God is I would also ponder how to get right with God. I knew Jesus had something to do with getting right with God. I knew that He died for my sin, but I didn't understand what that meant. I asked why anyone would give up their own life for someone else. I know I wouldn't give up my life for anyone else. What did all of this have to do with getting right with God anyway. I really didn't get why Jesus had to die on the cross.

In confirmation class I had to memorize the Apostles Creed. This Creed seemed to talk about God and Jesus. God was the Creator and Jesus was born of the Virgin Mary, was crucified, died and was buried. Then He came back from the grave and eventually went back to heaven. Right? I would find my confirmation notes so I could recite this creed. For some reason I always felt connected to this creed when it rolled off my lips.

I believe in God, the Father Almighty, maker of heaven and earth. And in Jesus Christ, his only Son, our Lord, who was conceived by the Holy Spirit, born of the virgin Mary ,suffered under Pontius Pilate, was crucified, died and was buried. He descended into hell. The third day he rose again from the dead. He ascended into heaven and sits at the right hand of

God the Father Almighty. From thence he will come to judge the living and the dead. I believe in the Holy Spirit, the holy Christian Church, the communion of saints, the forgiveness of sins, the resurrection of the body, and the life everlasting. Amen

This was just knowledge to me though, because I did not understand what it all meant. The question of who God is and how to get right with Him would frustrate me. Knowledge is something that anyone can obtain. Understanding is what I needed. All knowledge does is lead you to be superficial and shallow. It's a surface type of knowledge. I could impress others by quoting this creed in confirmation class, but I really didn't understand it. And I sure did not understand what the Scriptures said about who God is. But for some reason it was brought to my memory.

Good Deeds?

As I was thinking about a solution to getting right with God I thought since Jesus did His part then I have to do my part. And then this idea came to my mind. Maybe, just maybe, I could do enough good deeds to offset the bad deeds. You know, like balancing the scales so to speak. Do better and it will outweigh the bad right? That would surely make God happy. I've heard a lot of people say this, so it must be true. This made total sense to me. I was like 'I have the solution to my sin problem. Ok then, I'm gonna roll with this and figure it out.'

I heard someone say that they were working towards gaining points to get into heaven by doing good deeds. I thought 'Man, good deeds are something easy.' I felt relieved that it seemed very doable. I mean I was already a good guy so doing good deeds should come easy. God would have to let me in because I deserve it and I am a good person. That's logical. I'm good to go, I'm in! Right?

I started to think of good deeds I could do. The first one that came to mind is I could go to church. I remember talking to some of the guys I bowled with on a bowling league about this idea of going to church to gain points towards God. They told me they partied all week long and then showed up on Sunday and got a clean slate after confession. They would then say that they are good to go for another week of partying and whatever else they could find to get themselves in trouble.

I thought to myself that this is great. I can just do what I want and then show up on Sunday, do my part, go to confession and I'm good to go for another week. It would be like hitting the reset button. Going to church sounded like a good deed I could do. All I needed to do was find a church I could go to. I started to look in the phone book. Yes people, at one time you used to have to go to a phone book to find out where something was and the telephone number. That's what we did in 1991. I asked my bowling buddy where he went to church. He told me he went to the Catholic Church downtown. I was like "ohhh ok." I called the church the next day and asked about service times and what not. As I asked about going to confession and they told me that confession was for Catholic members only. I asked what it would take to be a member of the Catholic Church. They explained about needing to be baptized correctly and membership classes. I said thank you for your time and scratched that idea. It just sounded like too much work, there had to be good deeds easier than that to do.

I ask some people in a casual way what they did or would consider good deeds. There was this one person who went on about how he gives to charities every year. He said this made him feel good contributing to a good cause. He told me that he gave to the animal shelter, the soup kitchen and a local church where his wife attended. He chuckled as he said, "That should be enough charity," and then added "it should also be enough to get me a nice spot in heaven."

I started to think of charities I could give money to. I asked him how to find charities and how he went about finding his charities. He said look in the phone book. I did and found some places to call and start my giving to charity. The only thing was most every place I called wanted a commitment every month with a minimum amount. I was a bowling alley mechanic, and I didn't make much money. I couldn't afford to just give away my money. This just seemed too laborious for me, so I gave up on that idea.

I was brainstorming some more and the idea of volunteering at a soup kitchen came to mind. I went back to that phone book to find where there were some soup kitchens in the Flint Michigan area. I found one downtown that served the homeless.I thought this was perfect to gain points with God and this kind of good work should definitely get a good room in heaven.

I was all excited to do this thinking it would be my 'get into heaven' card. I called them to get the times I could volunteer only to find out that the time they needed people was during the time that I worked. My job didn't offer days off and to ask for one was not a good idea. This really bummed me out and I also lost hope that I could get into heaven through good deeds. What was I to do?

Pray?

What I thought was going to save me and get me into heaven was a dead end. I just couldn't figure it out. I mean, why was this so hard? I became more depressed and felt like there was no hope, like there was no way I was going to get it right with God. Why would God let me stay separated from Him? I don't understand why He wouldn't do anything to save me from hell. I was not a bad person. I did good things and was kind to others. **Yet, I felt like an outsider standing outside the door of the city walls.**

I just really felt like my life was over before it even got started. The carpal tunnel was destroying my bass player identity. Then, I felt like God rejected me. I just wanted to give up. I really did. To top that off I was so scared to die because I convinced myself I was hell bound. I just kept thinking about something happening to me and dying when I left the bowling alley after a night of shooting pool. I would always envision a truck T-boning me. Then of course my mind would run the scenario of what it would be like in hell. This would go on for days, maybe it was even weeks. The cycle would be bowl on the league, drink beer, end of the night agonizing over dying on the way home, then think what it will be like in hell. This was sending me to a nervous breakdown. I was beyond scared about this whole situation.

Then one night as this was going on that gut feeling came to me again and I heard a voice say- "Pray." I stopped what I was doing and had this blank stare on my face. I remember setting my beer down and I said out loud "Pray? To whom?" The voice said, "to God." I remember laughing and saying "are you kidding? Talk to God? Stop! No way!" I couldn't believe it. I didn't know how to pray to God. I remember praying in Sunday school as a kid and that was a lot of thank you prayers and "I hope grandma is ok" type prayers. What am I supposed to say?

It seemed weird to talk out loud to someone I can't see, I mean I might look crazy or something, right? I thought I might as well give it a try, what do I have to lose. I remember hesitantly starting to talk to God like He was a disappointed dad. I really thought he was mad at me or something. It took me a few times to start talking to Him but eventually I became comfortable and talked up a storm. I said the cliche statement 'God if You are real do something for me' prayer. I was ignorant and didn't know any better.

Then I was prompted to ask God for mercy. Must have been that inner gut again. I really didn't understand what I was asking of God when I asked Him for mercy. I sort of understood having mercy on someone, but I really didn't think God would actually have mercy on me. I ended up talking to Him about how I didn't understand how to get on his side and get to be heaven bound. How frustrating it was that I couldn't find a solution.

This type of prayer would go on for several nights. Then I started having encounters with what seemed to be angels as I would pray. It's like again there was a battle for my soul. That's the only way I can describe it. There were audible voices that would say "he is mine and you cannot have him." The other side really didn't say much, and I remember this feeling of being surrounded as if this other side was protecting me. I keep hearing a voice saying, “cry out to God and ask Him for mercy”.

After several nights of doing this there came a night, I felt that I was done praying this prayer. I remember feeling like I've done everything I could do, and it was out of my hands. Even though my carpal tunnel was in high gear, and I felt like my life was ruined, for the first time I felt a little peace. I actually felt something like goose bumps as I prayed for mercy.

“He saved us, not because of works done by us in righteousness, but according to his own mercy, by the washing of regeneration and renewal of the Holy Spirit,” Titus 3:5 ESV

God Came After Me

The Holy Spirit came after me and pursued me even though I was lost in my sin. He stirred up my heart with many questions and started a conversation within me. In my heart I had to come to an understanding about my sin condition and how this condition separated me from God. In doing this, it caused me to think about whether I am saved.

I was convinced that I was on my way to Hell, and because of that I became scared. Scared because in the afterlife there is no second chance. Once I'm thrusted into eternity- that's it, Heaven or Hell, no second chance at that point. No do overs! For whatever reason this concept was clear to me. I really believe it was the only way the Holy Spirit could get my attention.

So being scared I really didn't know any better, so I tried to fix it and figure things out on my own. I thought that maybe good deeds would be my ticket to heaven. That didn't work and it made me feel more lost and alone like there was no hope for me. I really didn't know what to do, I was at the end of my rope. Then the Holy Spirit prompted me to cry out to God for mercy. That's what I did.

I would keep searching as more questions would arise in my heart. I would continue to plead with God for mercy in the days ahead. While doing that, the Holy Spirit was very patient with me and would keep this conversation in front of me. **Sometimes we have to go through the process of thinking things through with the help of the Holy Spirit before we get to where we need to be. Thank you Jesus!**

Examples Of Good Works

There is a delusional teaching or philosophy today that we can earn our way to heaven by being a good person through merit, or good deeds. ***I'm***

here to tell you, you cannot earn your way to heaven by merit or good works. That is a false teaching. We cannot make our own path to heaven by being good and doing good works. This is what the world would want us to believe. The world tells us that we can do more good deeds than bad, and the scales will tip the way of good, and therefore proves we are a good person and deserve heaven. Does this sound familiar? The Bible does not teach this at all. The three actions of good works I thought about doing; going to church, giving money to charity, and doing community outreach went nowhere. ***The outwardly action of doing something good does not impress God. The inward condition of the heart is what God is concerned about.***

Let me expound on these ideas of good works for a minute. I've heard a lot of people say they need to go to church more to earn brownie points with God. To show they are putting in the time to assure their stairway to heaven is good to go. Good ole St. Pete will welcome them in because their church attendance meets the requirements. Right- and so when they go to church they can shake a few hands, put on their church smile, talk to a few people, sing some songs, and be on their way. Do you do this or know someone who does? If you do this, please stop. Go to church because you love Jesus, not to put on some kind of show. The action of going to church because you think it will earn your way to heaven is not in the Bible. Church is for fellowship and community. Church is a place to hear the Word of God. ***Church is not a social get together to show face***.

Another example of good work would be giving money to a charity. Give your money...and then tell everyone you gave money. For some reason we like to tell others about the money we just gave to charity. "Hey Jimbo, I was at church today and I threw 20 in the plate. So that's my good deed for the day, maybe even the month.' 'You know I gotta keep that stairway to heaven open.' Do you do this or know someone who does this? If you do this, please stop. Yes, we are supposed to give our money and time to the local church, but give because you love God, not to impress anyone. You cannot give your way into heaven. ***God doesn't want your money; He wants your heart.***

The last example is doing community outreach. If you are someone who does community outreaches, kudos to you. I think that is a great gesture for sure. Many of you may serve or have served at soup kitchens or food giveaways. Maybe you goto county jails and do Bible studies or do prison ministry and fellowship with inmates. Maybe you give your time and effort to help those who can't do their yard work, or you help them shovel their driveway. Whatever it is, I can't judge your motives. I can't say your actions are non-biblical. As a matter of fact, Jesus says that if you do these things to His people, you are doing it unto Him. *"Then the righteous will answer him, saying, 'Lord, when did we see you hungry and feed you, or thirsty and give you drink? And when did we see you a stranger and welcome you, or naked and clothe you? And when did we see you sick or in prison and visit you?' And the King will answer them, 'Truly, I say to you, as you did it to one of the least of these my brothers, you did it to me.'"* Matthew 25:37 ESV

But just know this, again, good deeds like all of these actions will not get you into Heaven. ***Actions of deeds do not bring salvation to anyone***. Because if you feed the hungry, give to the poor, clothe the naked, visit prisons with a 'look what I did motive' then it is for nothing. **Those actions are to be an overflow of your love for Jesus, not to be used as trophy points to earn your way to heaven.** ""Not everyone who says to me, 'Lord, Lord,' will enter the kingdom of heaven, but the one who does the will of my Father who is in heaven. On that day many will say to me, 'Lord, Lord, did we not prophesy in your name, and cast out demons in your name, and do many mighty works in your name?' And then will I declare to them, 'I never knew you; depart from me, you workers of lawlessness.'" Matthew 7:21-23 ESV

This world will come up with anything to keep you confused and frustrated. It will tell you that salvation is obtained by what you do. 'Do it yourself' is what the world tells you. Think about these three examples I gave you, what is the common thread with these three examples? 'I' and 'me' are common threads. 'I' went to church so people would notice 'me'. 'I' gave that money so people would notice 'me'. 'I' did all this community work so others would notice 'me'. If your motives are 'I' and 'me' then there is no salvation. ***Salvation is not our work; it is God Almighty's work. There is nothing we can do to earn salvation- nothing!*** *"For by grace you have been saved through faith. And this is not your own doing; it is the gift of God, not a result of works, so that no one may boast."* Ephesians 2:8-9 ESV

Crying Out For Mercy

As I look back on this moment this passage of scripture comes to mind "To some who were confident of their own righteousness and looked down on everyone else, Jesus told this parable: "He also told this parable to some who trusted in themselves that they were righteous, and treated others with contempt: *"Two men went up into the temple to pray, one a Pharisee and the other a tax collector. The Pharisee, standing by himself, prayed this: 'God, I thank you that I am not like other men, extortioners, unjust, adulterers, or even like this tax collector. I fast twice a week; I give tithes of all that I get.' But the tax collector, standing far off, would not even lift up his eyes to heaven, but beat his breast, saying, 'God, be merciful to me, a sinner!' I tell you, this man went down to his house justified, rather than the other. For everyone who exalts himself will be humbled, but the one who humbles himself will be exalted.""* Luke 18:10-14 ESV

Maybe, in a way, we are all like the tax collector in this passage of scripture. I know I felt like him. For someone to get to the point of asking for mercy it takes a road of frustration, struggle and confusion. I would say this tax collector knew he was separated from God and the only thing he knew to do was cry out for mercy. ***No one will cry out for mercy if they feel they have the solution to the problem***. In mine and the tax collector's case, we felt we could not come up with the solution to the problem. The problem being sin - The human condition or sinful nature. In other words, separation from the Presence of God Almighty. I can definitely identify with the tax collector. Just getting before God and sharing my heart was liberating for me.

Those who do not know Jesus are like the Pharisee. You could say I was like the Pharisee as well. I would directly or indirectly put others down around me like the Pharisee did to the tax collector. In my heart I thought that I was better than everyone. I was condescending and arrogant just like the Pharisee. Every time I felt guilt or shame for doing something wrong (sin) I would justify it so I wouldn't have to admit that I needed a Savior, just like the Pharisee did.

Having the heart of a Pharisee is pride with

the stench of arrogance. This heart condition will keep anyone from seeking God and His mercy which means there will be no forgiveness of sins. Having the heart of the tax collector, which was humility and broken, will perpetuate you towards God and His love, mercy and grace. I was a Pharisee, then the Holy Spirit showed me that I needed a Savior. I had to humble myself and look to God Almighty and cry out for Mercy to receive His Grace.

CHAPTER 9 "DRAWN TO HIS HEART"

God Pursues Me

God Answers

It was August 1991; I was barely getting through studio and rehearsals with Surreal and my wrists were not getting any better. I was still dealing with all this emotionally spiritual frustration of unanswered questions. But nonetheless I was still making an effort to keep doing music even though it was a tremendous challenge. Something had to give and hopefully soon.

During college I ended up making new friends. Many of us were performance majors and a few of us loved the music theory classes we took together. One particular friend I made a great connection with was Micah. Music theory class was our common ground but that would lead to a great friendship. We ended up writing writing a lot of music together.

One night Micah and I were on our way to hang out with a group of friends at a coney island restaurant and he told me there was someone he wanted me to meet.

I was curious, “That’s cool bro, can you give me a heads up of what this person is about?”

He said, “Sure! Her name is Regine and she is a foreign exchange student from former East Germany.”

I responded, “I dig man, look forward to it”.

We get to the restaurant, and I order my usual breakfast off the menu, and we are eating some food, having a good conversation and Micah grabs my attention to introduce me to Regine.

He said, “Mo, this is Regine "

I smiled and reached out my hand, “How do you do?”

We shook hands and she nodded her head towards me with a smile. I could tell she was overwhelmed by the circumstances with all the people around her. After all, she was from a foreign country still learning the English language and this group of people would be her friends for the next 11 months. She wanted to make sure she was accepted and fit in with all of us.

After Micah introduced us, I decided to strike up a conversation with her and try to get her to relax a little.

To break the ice, I asked her, “What is it like to live in Germany?”

She was happy to talk to me about her family and what life was like in Germany. I had, and still do, a genuine interest in the German culture so I was all ears. As a matter of fact, at the age of 5 I told my parents I wanted to learn German and be a German Pastor. They went out and bought me this book to start learning German. I think I still have it somewhere.

As we talked more that night, she became more comfortable, and I noticed myself becoming very drawn to her. She had a very easy-going personality and was very well mannered. I like being around people who are that way. But that wasn’t what was drawing me to her, what was drawing me to her was this peace that she had. As we talked, I just felt at ease. I didn’t really understand what it was or why I felt it, but all I knew is when I was talking to her that night, I experienced peace. It was like my whirlwind of feelings and emotions were put in check. I never experienced this before and I just knew it was drawing me in. Funny how I was trying to make her relax with conversation and she was actually making me relax with this unexplainable peace.

Towards the end of the night, we got on the topic of music. I asked her what type of music she liked.

She said to me, “You probably won’t know

what bands I like because they are German bands".

I said enthusiastically, "Tell me anyway, maybe I will recognize them".

She told me, and she was right, I didn't know them. Then she told me she liked classical music. This got my attention big time because I was studying music in college at the time. We talked about classical music for a while and some of the composers like Mozart, Bach, Beethoven and Gershwin. Then I told her I was a musician and asked if she played an instrument.

She said casually, "I do, I play violin".

My jaw hit the floor and I couldn't believe it.

"A violinist!" I said, "You're kidding?".

She said with a smile, "No, I'm not kidding".

I couldn't help but to chuckle about this and it was one of those "no way" moments. I went on to explain that I was at the beginning stages of recording an album in the studio and I wanted a violinist to be the main melody instrument throughout the album.

I have always loved music with the violin as the main instrument. Whether it be a violin concerto or carrying the main melody. My favorite composer for string instruments is Vivaldi, especially his amazing composition Four Seasons. The violin just captures all the feelings and emotions we experience as humans. It can be one of the most beautiful instruments in melody and then become one of the most intense and angry instruments at the drop of a hat. It can go from one end of the emotional spectrum to the other all in one song. And because of that, I had a love for the violin as being a lead instrument and was writing music specific for violin to be combined with a metal flavor.

But who would've thought that I would stumble onto a violinist at a coney island restaurant just hanging out. I was looking for a violinist for a while and could not find one at all. This was too good to be true that there was one right in front of me. I thought to myself "why not ask her to record this album with you." So, I asked her if she would want to work on this album with me and do some recording. I could tell she was flattered that I asked her but then she tried telling me that she may not be what I was looking for on violin.

I said to her, "Well can you play Bach's Sonata in C# minor, or Ave Maria?"

She replied, "Well yeah, I can play those pieces".

Then I said, "You will be just fine then with this music I'm working on."

She thought about it and then said, "Ok! Why not - Let's do this."

The stage was set, so to speak...

Let The Music Begin

The day came for our first rehearsal, and it

was nothing short of glorious. Things just fell into place real fast and everything she came up with fit great with the music and we just clicked. Her style of violin was a perfect match for the music that I was writing. The music was kind of a heavy metal meets classical music type of project so with her classical music violin training it worked really well. This would be my first attempt at writing music and recording an album. This was a musical steppingstone for me.

Anyway, I found out from some mutual friends that Regine was a Christian and she attended a church not too far from where I lived. When I heard this I was like "Ok this is interesting" and it got me thinking, "since she goes to church, maybe she could answer some of these questions I'm dealing with. I mean, after all she's a Christian, she should know this stuff". **Just know this, when people find out you are a Christian and go to church, they are going to expect you to know something about the Bible.**

At the time I found out she was a Christian there came a voice inside of me saying that I needed to talk to her. Not like an audible voice but rather a voice inside my mind. I have to admit a voice inside my mind was not an uncommon thing for me, but this time it was different. Instead of a voice encouraging me to fulfill the desires of my flesh it was encouraging me to spend time talking to someone about all of this emotional frustration and unanswered questions.

Also, at the same time, a feeling came over me wanting me to approach her and talk. It felt like a nudge more than anything. Do you remember when your parents would keep encouraging you to go over and talk to that new friend on the playground or maybe on a play date? I remember growing up I would be terrified meeting new friends. All kinds of things would go through my mind like, will they like me, will they make fun of me, will they accept me. In a nutshell I was dealing with the fear of rejection. I think all of us have dealt with the fear of rejection at some point in our life.

Because of this fear of rejection, I became nervous and scared of what might transpire if I did talk to her about all this penned up feelings and emotion inside of me. I thought "Maybe she would reject me or yell at me and call me stupid." Isn't it just like the devil to try to put fear inside of me and make me feel unworthy to talk to someone about God? The last thing the devil wants is for anyone to talk to a Spirit filled follower of Jesus Christ. The devil would put ideas in my head like "she doesn't want to talk to you about God", and "She'll pack her violin and leave, how embarrassing".

It was like a conversation of the little devil on one shoulder and a good guy on the other. Both of them are trying to persuade me to follow each one's line of thinking. Have you ever had a conversation like this? I remember seeing this play out in cartoons as a kid, oh the memories! The little devil side was loud and obnoxious, but the soft inward voice was the one that I was hearing more so than the other. It was saying to me "open up and share what you are feeling and ask the questions that are in your heart, she will listen".

Who Is God?

The next time we had rehearsal I eased into the conversation by telling her I heard she was a Christian and went to church. She said she was, and then told me what church she attended. Then I nervously asked her if it was ok for me to ask some questions about God and the Bible.

She said, "Sure, no problem".

After she said that she looked at me with this smile on her face waiting for me to ask a question. This was a huge relief, and it threw me off a little bit because I didn't expect her to be so open right away to the idea of talking about God.

I said, "Right now? I can ask you something...about God?"

She replied, "Yes, ask away!"

Even though I was nervous I thought to myself, 'Well, here it goes...'

I started with this question, "Who is God?"

She paused for a second and then she told me this,

"We cannot fully understand who God

is, but there are some things we can grasp," she continued, "God is so many things, like He is the Creator."

Then she went on to talk about how God is everywhere and in everything and told me to just look around at His creation and I can see God in it. She also explained that He is the Creator of the earth, moon, stars and all of the universe. As she expounded on God being the Creator it started to open my eyes and see the greatness of God. This was the beginning of the wheels in my head starting to turn. I started to think that maybe God really does exist.

I was taught this stuff in Sunday school, but Regine gave me a new way of looking at it. I mean, I love being outdoors and enjoying what nature brings me whether it be a cool fall day, or a thunderstorm, or a winter drive through the woods. Growing up my dad would take us up north a lot here in Michigan, and I learned to appreciate the very rich four seasons that Michigan offers. At the time I didn't see it through the idea of God being the Creator. Needless to say, we spent the rest of that rehearsal talking about how amazingly awesome God is as the Creator. The conversation continues.

The next day I found myself trying to find God in His creation. I remember staring at trees, grass, flowers and just taking in the blue sky and the fresh air. I felt goofy because I really didn't know what I was looking for, but I would still go outside and try to make the connection of God to creation. I can only imagine what I looked like from afar staring at trees with a dumb look on my face. Oh well, I didn't care what others thought.

When I got to the next rehearsal, I told her about me staring at the trees and the grass and she just simply encouraged me to not give up and keep searching. She could have laughed about it or made fun of me, but she did not do that. I thought that was pretty cool of her to not make me feel stupid. She knew I had knowledge from when I was a kid, but I was ignorant to the things of God. I was learning that I could trust her with my emotions and believe what she says is true.

What Is Sin?

We end up talking about this idea that God is Creator for the next few rehearsals but of course I have more questions burning inside of me. I asked her if it would be ok to ask other questions.

She again said, "No problem, go ahead."

By this time, I was feeling more comfortable around her and trusting her more and more with my emotions.

I asked, "What is sin?".

This question was a big deal for me because I knew that I was separated from God and was convinced that I was not going to heaven, which meant I was going to hell. I already went through all of the mental gymnastics to figure this out with no results. I told her that I would feel a sorrowful conviction that I am separated from God. I knew I wasn't right with God, and it had something to do with sin. I just didn't understand what sin was.

She answered my question with a question because she wanted to get my take on it first.

She asked me, "What do you think sin is?"

I really didn't know what to say other than,"Sin is when I do something wrong, I guess, I just know it is bad."

Then she asked me, "Can you give me an example of sin?"

The only thing I could think of was what I was taught in Sunday school, which was the 10 commandments like, don't lie, don't steal, don't kill anybody. I mean I had knowledge of this stuff but didn't understand it at all.

She listened to what I had to say with no judgment and

Then she looked at me and said, "Mike, if you are breathing then you are sinning."

I looked at her with this dumb look on my face and was like "huh?" I didn't know what she meant because again I was ignorant.

She went on to say that, "No matter how hard you try not to sin; you will still do it."

As I thought about what she said I was going back to the idea that I am a good person. I mean, I'm a likable guy, I get along with everybody and I really thought I treated people kindly.

I said, "I really don't do bad things that often, do I?"

She responded, "It doesn't matter what you do or don't do, you are a sinner by nature. It is this 'sin nature' that causes you to sin."

I asked her, "So I'm going to sin no matter what?"

She said, "Yes!"

In a strange way it was a relief to know that I am going to sin no matter what. I started to understand what it meant to be a sinner. That it wasn't necessarily a bad thing, but it took the pressure off me to not stress. My thinking was not to worry about it cuz I'm naturally going to sin. While she was in the USA, we would often talk about this question of what sin is. I didn't completely get it at the time, but I respected her and trusted that she was right.

She made reference to this Bible verse all the time when we talked about being a sinner by nature *"So now it is no longer I who do it, but sin that dwells within me. For I know that nothing good dwells in me, that is, in my flesh. For I have the desire to do what is right, but not the ability to carry it out. For I do not do the good I want, but the evil I do not want is what I keep on doing. Now if I do what I do not want, it is no longer I who do it, but sin that dwells within me."* Romans 7:17-20 ESV

Who Is Jesus? Clearly Hearing The Gospel

Talking about this idea of sin led right into talking about who Jesus is, and the Love of God. I'm just saying if you are going to tell someone that they are a sinner by simply existing then you might want to give them the solution to the problem of being a sinner. With this opportunity given to her Regine shared the life-changing Gospel of Jesus Christ with me.

She made it very simple for me and didn't complicate it with a lot of Scriptures and theology.

She started out by simply saying, "Jesus is the Son of God and He died for your sin", then she continued, "and because of that you are forgiven and set free from the bondage of sin and can now be in the Presence of God the Father."

I didn't really understand what she was saying but within my gut I wanted to hear more. Then she continued with a little fire in her and asked me, "Do you know why God sent Jesus to die for you?"

I thought about it and said, "Because I am a sinner?"

She replied, "Yes and we can do nothing to save ourselves from sin." She continued, "knowing that God's heart to send His only Son to die for our sin was motivated by His love for you and me," then she looked right at me and said, "God Loves you Mike... And because of this great love He has given you mercy and now you can have the free gift of grace."

This was to my knowledge the first time I heard the Gospel clearly.

Up to this point in my life no one spoke to me about the things of the Bible like she did. Everything she said to me I knew was right and it resonated with me. She spoke to me as one who was convinced that what she said was true. She was believable and had a strong conviction about her words. Her words were like a battering ram beating against the stone surrounding my heart and the stone was starting to crack.

I Am Loved?

Because she would always tell me that God loves I wanted to know what that meant. We were at another rehearsal getting ready to head in the studio.

I asked her, "What is the Love of God?"

She responded almost immediately with, "Unconditional".

I didn't know what she meant, so I asked her to explain.

She told me, "No matter what I do or say, whether it's right or wrong, God loves me no matter what my actions are." She went on to say, “If we do something wrong, we still have to be accountable for our actions and suffer the consequences, but God will still love us despite our wrongdoing.”

The conversation shifted from fear of the unknown to the idea that I am loved by God. She kept telling me that God loves me and cares for me no matter what I do or say. I couldn’t grab this concept that God loves me no matter what. That made no sense to me. I looked at love as being a performance thing. What can I do to make the other person happy? If I do something wrong and don’t measure up to their standards, then that other person would not love me as much. That was my thinking anyway.

I rationalized that if I do wrong all the time and don’t measure up then there is just no way that God loves me. I am a natural born sinner; I break the 10 commandments and other rules. I am always doing something wrong which means I am not measuring up to His standard. Again, how could God love me? I mean if I was God, I wouldn’t be able to love me O wretched man that I am. I just couldn’t wrap my mind around this concept. I really wanted to believe what she said was true.

I would be a terrible person at times when Regine and I would hang out. I would cuss up a storm and say really dumb offensive things. I would drag her around to all the things I wanted to do without much consideration of what she wanted to do. When we would hang outside of doing music, I would typically go pick her up and then take her to Colonial Lanes where we would shoot pool. She would put up with my rudeness and all the jokes that I thought were funny. She put up with a lot of my behavioral sin or wrongdoing. There was only one time she was annoyed with me and told me to tone it down. Which I did.

She accepted me even though I would act that way. She knew that everything I said and did was done out of ignorance and I didn't know any better. I was just acting like what I thought was right and normal. She didn't judge me or condemn me for my actions. By her accepting me and not crucifying me for my wrongdoing it opened the door for me to trust her. The words she spoke about God and the Bible would have an impact on me.

She really got me thinking about God's love for me and what that means. I asked the questions: what do you mean He had mercy on me, what is mercy? And what do you mean by the free gift of grace, what is grace? I didn't understand this, but I wanted to try and get it. We would have many conversations about the difference between God's mercy and God's grace. She would keep quoting me the Scriptures in Ephesians 2:4-5 *"But God, being rich in mercy, because of the great love with which he loved us, even when we were dead in our trespasses, made us alive together with Christ—by grace you have been saved*

—" Ephesians 2:4-5 ESV

A Gentle Spirit

'but in your hearts honor Christ the Lord as holy, always being prepared to make a defense to anyone who asks you for a reason for the hope that is in you; yet do it with gentleness and respect, ' 1 Peter 3:15 ESV

It was hard for me to get up the nerve to talk to Regine about God and the Bible. I didn't know what to expect or anything. If someone is asking you about God and the Bible pay attention and know this: that person more than likely has anxiety and is nervous about talking to you about God and the Bible. I know I was nervous because I didn't want to look stupid or be bulldozed with information and feel dumb for not knowing.

Regine could have told me so many other things of who God is. For example, God is love, God is merciful, God is our healer, God is our peace, God is our Redeemer, God is slow to anger, God is Steadfast, God is I Am, God is our everything, and so many more concepts of who God is. Instead, she shared something that I could relate to immediately, that being, God is our Creator. This really ministered to me and set the tone for what was to come. I encourage all of us to listen carefully to the leading of the Holy Spirit as we proclaim Christ Jesus to others.

You never truly know what is going through someone's mind when they approach you to talk about God. Remember at that moment they are letting their guard down and leaving themselves vulnerable to your reaction. It took a lot for me to put myself in that position. But I felt this peace about her, and I felt comfortable when we were together.

What I was feeling was the Holy Spirit in her drawing me in. One of the fruits of the Holy Spirit is peace (Galatians 5:22). She was a safe place, a strong tower, a place I felt I could rest my soul. It's the Holy Spirit that gives peace. As I felt comfortable talking to her the Holy Spirit was able to start ministering to me through her. She was the conduit that the Holy Spirit used to start proclaiming the Gospel to me.

She was ministering and because she was a Christian and studied the Word, she was equipped to do this work of God. And because she was equipped to do the work of God, she was able to give me a reason for the hope that was in her. She did it with gentleness and respect as the Scripture says *'but in your hearts honor Christ the Lord as holy, always being prepared to make a defense to anyone who asks you for a reason for the hope that is in you; yet do it with gentleness and respect,'* 1 Peter 3:15 ESV

She was very patient with me and was allowing me time to work it out in my head and did not expect me to understand this right away. Can I say it again- she was ***very patient*** with me. **Sometimes Christians just have to let the people around them work out their struggles and just be available while displaying the love of Christ.** That is exactly what happened. She just made herself available to answer questions I had and didn't judge me for not understanding right away.

I just want to point out that proclaiming the gospel is not all about the excitement of the miraculous. Like when Peter was preaching at Cornelius' house in Acts 10 and the Holy Spirit came into the house as he was preaching the gospel and filled everyone in the room with the evidence of tongues. Or when Paul in Acts 16 set a young girl free by casting out a demon of divination and was beaten and jailed for doing that.

There was no wow factor going on except me asking Regine questions and then she would simply answer them. I was a lost soul wandering in the wilderness searching for answers and looking for hope. It wasn't happening overnight but the more I spent time with her and asked questions the more my heart was being prepared to receive the good news of the Gospel. Which to me is a wow factor. Knowing how wicked the heart is and experiencing the preparation of my heart to receive the Gospel which is the greatest miracle.

Accepting Others

Patience with my sinful behavior was one thing but patience with my ignorance of the Gospel was another. I do not know how she endured my behavior and the things that came out of my mouth. Only through the doing of the Holy Spirit, I guess. Frustration can be a bigger challenge especially if you have to explain the same thing over and over. But she never showed frustration reexplaining things and for me not understanding the Gospel at first. It takes time for someone to understand with the heart (spirit) and because of her displaying patience through the Holy Spirit I was able to have time and not feel pressured to understand. She was just letting the Holy Spirit work it out within my own spirit. This approach to preaching the Gospel spoke volumes to me.

The reason it spoke volumes to me was because it made me feel *accepted* as a person not condemned as a sinner. **Patience leads to acceptance, and you cannot have one without the other. They both are critical in preaching the Gospel**. Condemnation has no place in proclaiming the Gospel of Christ Jesus. Let's take a look at an example of how Jesus handled a sinner caught in adultery.

"but Jesus went to the Mount of Olives. Early in the

morning he came again to the temple. All the people came to him, and he sat down and taught them. The scribes and the Pharisees brought a woman who had been caught in adultery, and placing her in the midst they said to him, "Teacher, this woman has been caught in the act of adultery. Now in the Law, Moses commanded us to stone such women. So what do you say?" This they said to test him, that they might have some charge to bring against him. Jesus bent down and wrote with his finger on the ground. And as they continued to ask him, he stood up and said to them, "Let him who is without sin among you be the first to throw a stone at her." And once more he bent down and wrote on the ground. But when they heard it, they went away one by one, beginning with the older ones, and Jesus was left alone with the woman standing before him. Jesus stood up and said to her, "Woman, where are they? Has no one condemned you?" She said, "No one, Lord." And Jesus said, "Neither do I condemn you; go, and from now on sin no more."]]" John 8:1-11 ESV

There is so much to this passage of Scripture. First, according to the Law of Moses this woman was supposed to receive death by stoning for her action of adultery. In other words, the Pharisees found her guilty and condemned her. When they brought her to Jesus, they expected Him to follow their line of thinking and agree that she should be executed by stoning.

Instead, He does something unexpected, He shows mercy and looks past the sin of this woman and goes to her defense. Jesus bends over to draw in the sand and some scholars say He was writing the sin of each Pharisee out in the sand for all to see. Then He says, "Let him who is without sin among you be the first to throw a stone at her." Not one Pharisee could say anything after Jesus said that because all of them knew they had sin in their heart as well. One by one they all walked away. After that, Jesus turns to the woman and does something amazing. He does not judge her or condemn her but instead accepts her where she was at, sin and all, and He shows her unconditional love, mercy, compassion, and then forgives her. That is amazing! Jesus did not deal with her according to the laws of condemnation, but instead, reacted with love.

Now, think about what could have been going through this woman's mind. I mean she is dragged to Jesus and accused of adultery, and she is probably sure she will face death - Again hear these words of Jesus in verse 11 - *Jesus stood up and said to her, "Woman, where are they? Has no one condemned you?" She said, "No one, Lord." And Jesus said, "Neither do I condemn you; go, and from now on sin no more."]]"*

Jesus loved the woman who was caught in adultery, which created the compassion to give her mercy instead of her consequence, which then led to the free gift of grace by forgiving her and encouraging her to sin no more. Love, Mercy and Grace. Just as the Scripture she quoted to me often in Ephesians 2:4-5.

There were many opportunities for Regine to cast stones at me, but she didn't. Instead, she showed the love of God to me by looking past my sin and being compassionate just like Jesus was to the woman caught in adultery. We are *all* this woman if you think about it.

I cannot emphasize enough how **accepting someone where they are at, is a part of preaching the Gospel.** If you look at the word acceptance in the dictionary, we find that it is actually an ***action*** word. The Bible calls us to love with actions and in truth. You could say that acceptance is love in action.

The battering ram of the Word of God continued to beat against the wall of stone around my heart. It was like each time she answered a question I could feel something inside of me cracking these walls of my pride. **The worldview and the culture of our day will mold the way we think and act**. Like what I mentioned earlier, the ways of the world: the lust of the flesh, the lust of the eyes and the pride of life do everything they can to keep God and Jesus Christ out of everything and everyone.

I could feel the tension inside of me as I wrestled with this idea of God's love. Then the Holy Spirit showed me an example of this love that was right in front of me. My Mom and Dad continually showed me the love of God throughout my life. Today, it's just my Mom, as my

Dad is with Jesus now. Love you, Dad!!

The Holy Spirit showed me how they loved me despite all of my mistakes. My parents were not perfect people who had it all figured out, none of us do, but they were able to look past my selfish actions and not treat me how my actions deserve. My Dad told me one time, "**We are imperfect people trying to love imperfect people**". What he meant by that was we all make mistakes and need to realize that we are all imperfect and then put that line of thinking into action with the idea of love.

I could go through my list of mistakes and how I mistreated people including my parents. I guess we could each get our list of mistakes and stare and compare our lists. I don't know what good it would do to look at each other's faults but that is what we naturally do with each other. Our example is Jesus and how He handled the woman caught in adultery. Love, mercy, grace with compassion, and forgiveness.

I encourage you to take a moment right now to think of someone who is in your sphere of influence who needs acceptance instead of condemnation, who needs compassion instead of unreachable standards. Now, pray for that person, and believe God to give you the opportunity to proclaim the Good News of Jesus Christ to them.

CHAPTER 10 "VICTORY"

Darkness Will Not Overcome

Invited To Church

While Regine was here in the USA, she was invited to speak at different churches in the area about her experience growing up behind the Berlin wall. The opportunity came for her to speak about this at her home church, Calvary United Methodist Church in Flint, Michigan. She invited me to come hear her speak and of course I said yes.

I started to stress out over what I was going to wear to this church service. I think it was more because I haven't been to church in forever and I wanted to make a good impression to her host parents and church family. I really couldn't afford a suit and then I remembered my suit from my confirmation celebration. I went home and dug out this suit from my closet. It was a grayish blue suit and needless to say it was a little tight, but it would have to do for this occasion.

Sunday came to go to her church and hear her speak. As I was getting ready that morning, I was feeling uneasy. I thought maybe I was just nervous or something after all I haven't been to church in quite some time. I kicked around the idea of not going at all. It was unusual for me to feel sick at all. I normally don't deal with feeling sick. Back and forth I went as to whether I should go or not. I didn't want to let Regine down, so I finished getting ready.

When I got to the church, I parked my car and wanted to take a minute to pull myself together. I start tapping my head on the steering wheel saying to myself "I can do this...I can do this, right?" Took a couple deep breaths and sat in silence for about a minute. I thought "ok...I think this uneasy feeling is not going to bother me now." I get out of my car and start walking inside the church.

As I'm walking into the church this uneasy feeling starts up again and intensifies. I turn around to get back in my car and go home. But something inside me changed my mind and next thing I know I'm walking into that church. As soon as I stepped my foot inside, I broke out in a sweat, my heart was pounding, and I couldn't relax and be myself. I had an intense feeling of that

I didn't want to be there at all. I couldn't figure out what was wrong with me because I'm a laid-back guy and there is no reason for me to feel this anxious at all.

I shook a few hands when I got there and then I eventually found Regine. She looked at me and asked me if I was, ok?

She said, "You are sweating and white as a ghost."

I explained to her what was going on and she just looked at me and smiled, gave me a hug,

And she said, "If you need to go home, I understand."

I told her I would let her know. She nodded and went about her way of other people wanting to talk to her.

I eventually calmed down enough to find a seat after going outside a few times for fresh air. I remember closing my eyes and saying, 'this will only take an hour and then it will be over'. Her host parents sat next to me, and they made small talk with me which made me feel a bit more comfortable. I was still very anxious and uneasy, but I finally felt calm enough to stay and listen. I really wanted to hear what she had to say. It was like something would not let me leave the church.

The service started, and I started becoming more relaxed. The music was great, and I was breathing easier. I didn't see Regine as the service was going on and I wanted to make sure she knew I was there before she started talking. As she was walking up to the pulpit, I was able to catch her eye to let her know I was there. When she started to speak, I was all ears. And lo and behold I didn't feel uneasy at all when she was speaking.

She told her story of what life was like living behind the Berlin wall and how there were challenging times for her and her family. Then she talked about what life was like after the wall came down, how there was a victory and the freedom she gained. She compared that to the Scriptures and talked about us being free in Christ and how He can break down the walls in your heart. It was a great message and when she was done, she received a standing ovation.

The service ended and of course people surrounded her, wanting to talk to her. They were giving her high fives and accolades for doing such a good job. Once the service was done that anxious feeling reared its ugly head again, and this time it was quite strong. I just couldn't wait to get out of there. I shook a few hands and told her I would meet her out in the parking lot when she was done.

As I was walking to the doors, I could just feel some kind of battle going on. I could hear battle sounds and vocal grunts as I was walking out. As soon as I walked through the double doors and stepped foot in the parking lot the overwhelmingly uneasy anxious feeling disappeared. It was like I stepped into normal again and there was not one hint of being uneasy.

It was like someone took a heavy blanket off of me and I didn't feel trapped and suffocated anymore.

I remember looking around outside and asking myself what just happened. I thought 'All morning I felt overwhelmed and uneasy and in an instant that feeling was gone.' Like the snap of my fingers- gone! I thought about what just happened for a few minutes. Then I took a deep breath as I looked up to the sky and an indescribable peace came over me. I had no idea what was going on. It felt like something ended, like a battle was over and done.

Prayer

As I stood there in the parking lot with this amazing stillness in my heart, I took another deep breath and gathered my thoughts. I remember I was exhausted after this service. My body felt tired like I just got done doing an intense workout. There was a sense of new beginnings like there was something new coming my way. It's like I had a feeling to leave the past way of thinking in the past. I didn't have any idea of what to expect. All I knew is I was peacefully exhausted, so I sat outside waiting for Regine to come out.

It was alright that it took her a while to come out, because I had to 'take it in' and recover from what just happened to me. I wasn't concerned about what I'll call a notable spiritual battle that went on around me. In my gut I knew there were demons and angels around me, and I believe that Sunday service they were engaged in a battle over whether I would show up or not.

What was more notable that Sunday was the still peace I had walking out those church doors and into the parking lot. I remember looking up to the sky and seeing this wonderful display of sunlight coming through the clouds. I wish I had a camera that day because it was amazing. During this experience of peace, I remember having a sense that God was around me and protecting me. There were no words spoken but I guess you could say I felt like I was in a place of rest.

I really felt as though God fought for my soul that day and that He was there with me in that parking lot. I raised my arm to the sky and started to talk to God. I had such gratitude in my heart. My emotions were everywhere at that time, and I just remember bursting into tears because I felt free. I didn't know what I was free from, but I just know I felt different. The feeling that God loves me came to me as I was in tears. I don't know why I would think that but for some reason I started to think that "maybe God does love me."

Regine finally made her way out of the church. By this time, I'm sitting in my car resting my eyes. When I saw her, I gave her a hug and told her what a great job she did with her message. She could tell something was different about me, so she asked me what was going on.

I said, “Hey let's go grab something to eat and I’ll tell ya what happened today.”

Of course, she said yes.

On our way to eat I explained everything that happened. From the uneasy overwhelming feeling that almost kept me from coming to the service, to the amazing peace when I got into the parking lot and everything in between. I told how I felt like there was a battle for my soul, and that I had feelings that “maybe God does love me.” I was getting excited about God, and she could see that.

I found a parking spot and put the car in park.

She looked at me and said, “Since the day we started hanging out I have not stopped praying for you.”

She went on, “I have been praying for you and against the forces of evil around you and it’s been a battle with strong resistance.”

I said, “You really pray for me like that?”

She said “Yes! And because sometimes the resistance is strong, I become tired some days because it takes a lot out of me to pray.”

It was at that moment that I realized that God does love me. She confirmed all of the things that I was hesitant to believe. Everything that I was feeling - the battle, the peace, the love. It was all real and of God, genuinely. As we went inside to eat, we talked more about God, and I had an inward peace all night long. We ended up sharing a banana split sundae, then I took her home.

I Am Reconciled

The next few days I would spend time thinking about this journey, and how carpal tunnel was trying to destroy my bass identity. All of this prompted conversations within me. Conversations like heaven and hell, sin and separation, God and His love, mercy and grace. I realized that the questions I searched for were starting to be answered. All of this was starting to make sense to me.

Even though the carpal tunnel was still in my wrists, it did not dominate my thought life anymore. I couldn't pinpoint when that started to happen. All I knew is my identity as a bass player was not as important to me as it used to be. I arrived at a point where I felt if I played bass for a living then that would be great. If not, then so be it. Of course, my heart's desire was to see this carpal tunnel go away, but there were just more important things I wanted to see happen in my life. I had a peace that everything would be ok.

I pondered the idea of heaven and hell. When I was asking the question as to whether or not hell is real, I came to realize that it really is a place of separation from God. And then this caused me to believe that heaven was real as well. As I thought about this it led to the question of who God is and what is sin, I would ponder what the conversations were, and the way that Regine answered these two questions.

Who is God? When I asked that question her response was something I could instantly relate to. I thought about how she was able to get me to focus on God being the creator. As I would think about God as my creator it made me see God in a different way. I literally would stare into the sky and ponder the greatness of what I was seeing. My dad helped with that as well because he would always reference God's creation.

What is sin? When I asked that question her response was if you are breathing then you are sinning. I'll never forget that. I was starting to understand what that means. The two concepts I was learning were: I couldn't do anything about the sin condition, and I couldn't save myself by earning anything with God. But I started to think that God has to be bigger than my sin. After all, He created the skies and sun and the whole earth and everything in it.

As I continued to think about this concept, I couldn't help but to ask the question of how God could love a sinner like me. I thought about how God came to my defense at Regine's church and fought the battle in the spirit realm that was going on. To me, I was amazed because I didn't ask God to do that. He just showed Himself that day and made sure I was at that service. For me it was that feeling that God cared and without me asking He did something amazing. It was God Almighty sticking up for me and taking on the bully who is pushing me around. To me, that action of sticking up for me showed me that He loved me.

Then I was reminded of the conversations Regine and I would have about God's mercy and grace. She would always talk about how Jesus died for my sin and by His blood it is taken away. She would say things like “you are washed clean,” “He saved you,” “your sin is forgiven.” And Jesus seemed to be the person who was doing the washing, saving and forgiving. I concluded that after pondering all these things I had to find out who Jesus is.

I called Regine the next day and set a time we could get together and talk more about God and the Bible. we met on Wednesday of that week at Colonial Lanes after she got out of school. We went inside and I rented the pool table and started to put my pool cue together so we could play 9-ball. We were just making small talk about our day and some of the music we were working on together.

We get into a game of 9-ball, and for some reason I am nervous about talking to her about who Jesus is. I just felt that this was a super important thing to talk about. We shot pool for a bit and my nerves calmed down and I was able to start talking about the things we have been discussing for months. I just wanted to do a summation of everything we talked about.

Then I said, “Alright, well I want to ask you

another question,"

She replied "Ok, what is it?"

I was sitting in a high bar stool in the pool hall, and I looked right at her and asked, "How do I get to know Jesus?"

She paused and took a step back and looked at me with this look of 'it's about time you asked me that' and started smiling.

I remember she put her hands on my shoulders and looked me in the eye and said, "You just need to believe Jesus died on that cross for your sin that He was buried and was raised from the dead."

Then she asked me, "Do you believe that Mike?"

I said, 'Yes I do."

Then she asked me, "Is Jesus now the Lord of your life?"

I said, "Yes He is."

She then said, "Because you believe in your heart that God raised Jesus from the dead and confess Him as the Lord of your life - you are saved."

My heart was cut by what the Holy Spirit was saying through her. Tears started rolling down my face and the Holy Spirit convicted me to repent and ask my Lord Jesus to forgive my sin. So right there in the pool hall of Colonial Lanes I repented and asked Jesus to forgive me and to wash me clean. Regine wanted to pray with me right there. With tears streaming down my face and a joy unspeakable in my heart she grabbed my hands and prayed. She thanked God and asked Him to strengthen me and grow my faith. She thanked Him for setting me free. I just know when she was done praying the Presence of God was evident, and joy and peace overwhelmed me in that room.

After she was done praying, I didn't know what to do with myself. It was like all my questions were answered and all these feelings and emotions I was dealing with were put to rest. I thought "God really does love me, and His Son Jesus really did die for my sin, and now my sin is gone -- I am free, He has set me free." I was free indeed. The burden of sin was lifted. Praise the Lord!!

God's Presence Heals

After we were done praying, I got out of my stool and started to walk around the pool hall. I couldn't believe what just happened.

I said to her, "Come on, let's go for a walk."

We started walking around the bowling alley for a bit. We didn't say much to each other, but just kept smiling and taking in what God just did and was continuing to do. I had tingling goosebumps and could not shake the joy and peace I was experiencing.

There was a hallway off to one side of the

pool room that we started to walk down. As we walked down there, I could feel God's presence started to take over me. Not just a feeling in my mind anymore but instead my whole body physically started to feel His presence. While this was happening, the Holy Spirit gave me this idea in my spirit that I wanted to play my bass for God and glorify His Name.

I remember getting bummed out though because I didn't know how I was going to be able to do this with my carpal tunnel. I mean not too long before this I had to drop out of college because of this medical condition. The doctor's said surgery was the only option. My hands were so weak at times I couldn't even grip a coffee mug. We did this thing where I would squeeze her index finger as a way to gage how strong my hands were that day. You could say I failed every time because usually there was no strength in my hands.

I had all this on my mind, but the Presence of God would not let up and the Holy Spirit kept stirring up in my spirit this desire to commit my bass talent to Him. With all the negative thoughts of my carpal tunnel it seemed impossible to commit my talent to God. In my mind there was no talent to give. I didn't know what to say or how to approach God about this while in this moment of God's presence. I didn't understand faith, or how to pray, or how to do anything according to the Word of God. But the Holy Spirit kept nudging me to approach God.

I just said the first thing that came to my mind, "God, I just know I want to play my bass for You, but I can't, because I have this carpal tunnel."

Then I said, "If you don't do something about it, I'll just go back to school and...."

No sooner than that came out of my mouth the Almighty God interrupted me with something totally unexpected. All of a sudden, the presence of God started to intensify throughout my whole body, and it was burning in my wrists. Both my wrists felt like they were on fire. This hit me like a freight train. I started crying tears of joy and laughing from feeling so happy. Then the presence of God became heavier over me like it was knocking me to my knees. I couldn't fight it and I was hoping it would not end. I looked at Regine and asked her if she could feel what I was feeling. She said she couldn't feel something, but she could tell something was going on with me.

In the middle of this encounter with God Almighty I asked her to stick out her index finger, you know, to do 'the test'. I grabbed a hold of it and about broke her finger as I squeezed it. It was at that point I realized that the carpal tunnel was gone from my wrists and hands. I couldn't believe what was going on. My God, Jehovah-Rapha, my healer physically healed my carpel tunnel and completely restored my strength. I was jumping for joy and with clenched fists as I raised my hands to the sky. I couldn't calm down. I kept going outside, then back inside, and I just couldn't stop being excited and overjoyed for what the Lord had done. The carpal tunnel was gone and I was, and still am, healed. Hallelujah!! Praise the Lord!!

It Took Only One

"For he has rescued us from the dominion of darkness and brought us into the kingdom of the Son he loves, in whom we have redemption, the forgiveness of sins." Colossians 1:12-14 NIV

It only took one person to invest their time and life into one person to make that difference Regine was that one person that God Almighty chose to use and make a difference in my life and be a vessel for the Holy Spirit to do His work. She was obedient to the things the Holy Spirit put on her heart to do and speak. And because of that I can say with confidence that I am a Blood bought child of the Most High and I am Heaven bound. **It only takes an army of one who is backed by the army of Heaven to change someone's life for Christ Jesus!**

She only had the Holy Spirit to lead her and prompt her when to pray and then give her words to speak into my life. I say that to encourage us to understand God can use anyone at any time to do His will. Whether it's an army of one or an army of many. She just did what she thought was right and tried her best to be available to display

God's love. Then when the Holy Spirit opened the door for her to share the Word of God, the Gospel, she shared it with boldness and allowed the Holy Spirit to do the work.

She did not change me or save me, the blood of Christ crucified preached is what changed me and saved me. She did not heal me of my carpal tunnel, the Presence of God is what healed me. She was just a willing ambassador of Christ Jesus willing to be obedient to the Holy Spirit's leading. My life was forever changed by the Good News of the Gospel of Christ Crucified!! Hallelujah!!!

I was once in the darkness and my heart was blinded by the god of this world. Now I am in the Kingdom of light, the kingdom of the Son he loves. I am so, so grateful for Christ Jesus rescuing me from the pit of hell and putting me on the Rock, not sinking sand. He redeemed my life, and He forgave me and saved me from the condemnation of hell. *"For he has rescued us from the dominion of darkness and brought us into the kingdom of the Son he loves, in whom we have redemption, the forgiveness of sins."* Colossians 1:12-14 NIV

God Fought For Me

That Sunday morning when I went to hear Regine preach at Calvary United Methodist

Church, there was an obvious battle going on. I didn't really recognize that until the service was done, and I was in that parking lot. I didn't say a word because I didn't know what to say. I didn't understand anything of the Word of God on how to pray or stand on the Word. Yet, the Lord of Host's fought this battle for me and made it known to me that He fought that battle. Like the Scripture says, *"The Lord will fight for you, and you have only to be silent.""* Exodus 14:14 ESV

The Lord allowed me to physically feel this battle for a reason. I just felt the pull back and forth of something wanting me to leave and not attend this service.God used what the devil was trying to do to show me something. God Almighty showed me that He loves me by not allowing the devil to have his way by keeping me from going. It was like God was sticking up for me and keeping the bully, that being the devil, from pushing me around. He is the one who stood in my defense, He is the one who kept encouraging me to go hear Regine preach.

You see I did not feel worthy of God's love or feel I deserve anything from Him. I was lost and blind, dead in my sin so why would he even give me the time of day. Well, He did give me the time of day and because of that alone I realized He loved me. Why would He even come to my defense if He didn't didn't have some sort of love for me. This was a big deal to me because I didn't have to ask Him to fight for me, He just showed up and made it happen and allowed me to know that He made it happen.

God does come to the defense of those who cannot defend themselves. He comes to the aid of those in need.The parable of the lost sheep I think is fitting. "But the Pharisees and the teachers of the law muttered, *"And the Pharisees and the scribes grumbled, saying, "This man receives sinners and eats with them." So he told them this parable: "What man of you, having a hundred sheep, if he has lost one of them, does not leave the ninety-nine in the open country, and go after the one that is lost, until he finds it? And when he has found it, he lays it on his shoulders, rejoicing. And when he comes home, he calls together his friends and his neighbors, saying to them, 'Rejoice with me, for I have found my sheep that was lost.' Just so, I tell you, there will be more joy in heaven over one sinner who repents than over ninety-nine righteous persons who need no repentance."* Luke 15:2-7 ESV

I was that lost sheep. I was wandering around defenseless and could in no way defend myself. If a wolf came to me and it was just the two of us, that wolf would tear me to pieces. But God never allowed me to be torn to pieces by the wolves, Satan's demons, while I was out wandering in the wilderness. I have to believe that he protected me even though I was not saved.

This protection allowed the Good Shepherd, Jesus, to come and find me. I was lost, wandering, there was no way I would survive out in the wilderness on my own. I didn't know how to defend myself against the wolves. I didn't know what to do if I slipped on a rock and broke a leg. Sheep are defenseless- I was defenseless. I was easy prey for Satan to come and devour me.

I have to say the Good Shepherd showed up that day at Calvary United Methodist. He kept the wolves back and started to bring me back into the flock. I had such peace from that parking lot to my carpal tunnel being healed. Like I said I felt like there was a battle won and I was exhausted like I just worked out. Like the battle that day took the strength out of me. The Good Shepherd fought my battle and then carried me back home.

Motivated By Love

When I thought about why the Good Shepherd would come after a lost sheep, I could only draw one conclusion. That the Good Shepherd loves the lost sheep. He could let that lost sheep go and say, "well that one wandered off on their own and I will just cut my loss and tend the other 99." No instead He says, "I love that sheep and I need to go and get him and bring him home."

Ezekiel 34 prophesies about this very thing. He makes the point that the sheep are scattered because of abusive misleading shepherds (Pharisees). And because of that they have no shepherd. God says in the prophecy, ""*For thus says the Lord God: Behold, I, I myself will search for my sheep and will seek them out. As a shepherd seeks out his flock when he is among his sheep that have been scattered, so will I seek out my sheep, and I will rescue them from all places where they have been scattered on a day of clouds and thick darkness. I myself will be the shepherd of my sheep, and I myself will make them lie down, declares the Lord God. I will seek the lost, and I will bring back the strayed, and I will bind up the injured, and I will strengthen the weak, and the fat and the strong I will destroy. I will feed them in justice."* Ezekiel 34:11-16 ESV

So the Sovereign Lord said he would search for the sheep. He said that He would rescue them from the scattered mountains and then tend to the sheep. We are His children and when we are lost, He is going to come find you. He will pursue you. Why?? Like I said, because He loves you. He sends the Good Shepherd out in the dangers of the wilderness to bring home the lost sheep. I was a lost sheep, but He came and found me. I was in the wilderness not knowing what to do and He stood up for me and protected me from the wolves. His motivation was love.

Then Mercy...

Because of this great love for me I was able to obtain mercy. Mercy is something that I do not deserve. *"he does not treat us as our sins deserve or repay us according to our iniquities."*Psalms 103:10 NIV

God did not have to extend His mercy to me at all because I am a sinner saturated with sin. I couldn't come into His presence as a sinner - I would die. He is a Holy God.

Even though we do not deserve mercy the Scriptures say that He is a merciful God. *"The Lord is merciful and gracious, slow to anger and abounding in steadfast love."* Psalm 103:8 ESV After the Good Shepherd found me and I was able to experience mercy. Jesus didn't punish the sheep He found for leaving the flock. He didn't say "you broke your leg? Good! You deserve it." Or say "You're hungry? Well, you shouldn't have left the flock in the first place." Those responses are not of the Sovereign God.

That's not how He treats us when we are found. No! He tends to our wounds, feeds us and gives us drink. How many of us can say we have had, or still have, a wounded spirit who hungers and thirsts for salvation. He told us that He is the Bread of Life and anyone who eats this Bread will be hungry no more. He calls us on to drink of the water He has, and we will thirst no more. He promises us that he will mend the broken-hearted. In other words, Mercy.

He won't leave us to endure what we deserve. If He was to do that He would contradict His Word and He would be a hoax. But God is a merciful God who loves us. That love he has for us the root for His mercy. He has been giving me mercy since the day I was born. I was born a sinner so therefore I have needed His mercy since that day and because He loves me, I have been in His mercy.

Then Grace...

Because of God's great love for me I was able to obtain mercy which then I was able to receive the free gift of grace. That night at the bowling alley I received the free gift of grace. The Holy Spirit opened my heart to hear the Good News of Grace- Christ crucified. It cut to my heart then I repented of my sin, and I believed Christ Jesus was raised from the dead and I confessed Christ Jesus as my Lord for the first time.

Mercy: God does not give us the punishment we deserve. Grace: God gives us the gift we do not deserve. The thing about mercy is the one giving the mercy also has the authority to be unmerciful. Also, the fact that grace is of God, means we cannot earn grace by works. Which then means salvation is not our work, rather it is the work of the Lord Almighty and Him alone.

Once I received the free gift of grace that night in the bowling alley God confirmed His word with healing of my carpal tunnel.This healing is His work and His work only. I didn't ask for it and

I didn't deserve it. Yet God in His love, mercy and grace gave me healing in my body. The Glory goes to Him and Him only. Hallelujah! I am redeemed by the Blood of the Lamb. I am reconciled and made a new creation, because He who knew no sin became sin for me. Praise the Lord!!

If you notice throughout my story of reconciliation, I didn't do anything to earn God's love. I didn't force Him to love me, He just loves me. I didn't do anything to deserve God's mercy. Because of His love for me mercy was able to triumph. I didn't do anything to earn God's grace. It is a free gift of God. Read this Scripture over and over to understand the heart of the Gospel. In Jesus Name…Amen.

EPILOGUE

"But God, being rich in mercy, because of the great love with which he loved us, even when we were dead in our trespasses, made us alive together with Christ—by grace you have been saved—"
Ephesians 2:4-5 ESV

The Threefold Mercy of the Gospel:
LOVE, MERCY, and **GRACE**
Because of God's great **LOVE** for me
I was able to obtain **MERCY**,
which allowed me to accept
His free gift of **GRACE**.
~Michael Jones

To find out more about Michael "Mo" Jones and his music, visit MoJonesBass.com

ABOUT THE AUTHOR

Michael 'Mo' Jones

Michael Jones is an American award-winning bass player and musician who resides in Flushing, Michigan. Michael has a Bachelor's Degree in Biblical Studies with an emphasis on Evangelism from Liberty University. He has been an Evangelist for over 30 years spreading the Good News of Christ Crucified. In doing this, he has seen many come to the saving knowledge of Christ Jesus and experience the amazing love of God Almighty. Michael was given the stage name of "Mo" Jones. Mo has offered his bass playing skills to several ministries and churches over the years. He has also recorded his signature bass style on several albums for different artists over the last 40 plus years. Within that timeframe he wrote, recorded, and produced two albums of his own band Threefold Mercy: Only Love Remains (1995)

and My Hope Is In You (2017). Focusing on his bass skills he also wrote, recorded, and produced two solo bass albums: Mo Jones Bass (2007) and Bassin (2010). He continues to write and record music. To find out more about Michael "Mo" Jones and his music, visit: MoJonesBass.com

Made in the USA
Middletown, DE
23 October 2023

41225731R00136